Agglomerate

from idea to IPO in 12 months

JEREMY HARBOUR and CALLUM LAING

As a champion for growth and ambition, Nasdaq congratulates the continued success of The Marketing Group after its successful IPO on First North.

The Marketing Group is among the many global companies listed on Nasdaq First North that have gone on to grow, innovate, and deliver great returns for their investors.

Nasdaq is proud to be the listing partner of The Marketing Group and looks forward to its continued growth in the future.

Nelson Griggs,
Executive Vice President of Listings Services at Nasdaq

Praise

"This great book doesn't just comprehensively bust and de-bunk the myths of the entrepreneurial journey, it gives us a seriously fresh way of creating value. Simply brilliant and an absolute must read."

Paul Dunn, Chairman, Buy One Give One, www.b1g1.com

"*Agglomerate* is a hard hitting book that reveals the ugly truth behind entrepreneurship – slogging long hours for pittance, running out of funds, etc, which other business books tend to sweep under the carpet. Jeremy and Callum offer a game-changing concept, which, if executed well, could be the lifeline for many businesses."

Pearlin Siow, author, *Boss Of Me* (www.bossofme.sg)

"Having been selling small engineering companies for the last 10 years, it has become increasingly difficult as they are too small for the 'big boys' and the 'small boys' don't have the cash. Also, the price expectation of the seller is way out of line with reality. The Agglomeration model fixes all these issues and gives the owners/shareholders both scale and liquidity. This model has formerly only been open to the 'big boys' who pay massive advisory fees. Now it's open to much smaller enterprises."

Chris Cundy, Techsearch M&A.

"Truly revolutionary thinking on how to increase wealth and change the world. The model that Callum and Jeremy have designed is robust and proven. The book is written for entrepreneurs by entrepreneurs and will change the way you look at businesses and wealth creation. A must read for every budding businessman and investor!"

Rajesh Nair

"Agglomeration is a great new concept that solves many problems for small business owners: talent retention, succession planning, liquidity, value creation, the scale paradox and more. It works particularly well when agglomerating geographically diverse similar businesses, as the authors have already proven with their The Marketing Group project."

Hans Kull, Managing Director, InMatic

"You'd better read this book and do it fast, because it shows ways to increase shareholder value. Entrepreneurs needs this book; it is a gem. The ideas, strategies and tactics are all used in making real deals. Jeremy Harbour and Callum Laing are changing the game of entrepreneurship."

Goran Pregelj, Investor in SMEs globally

"It's sad but true. Many entrepreneurs go into business thinking that it'll give them more time and more money, but it takes up all their time and all their money.

We are envious of those entrepreneurs who made it big – either by raising tons of money or selling their businesses for tons of money. How do they do it?

Agglomerate is a no-holds-barred book. It is going to bust some myths about entrepreneurship while providing ground-breaking, insightful knowledge and ideas of how to make more wealth. You will be thinking hard while, and long after, you read this book."

LayYong Ooi, Co-founder, BodyTree GST –
a gymnastic strength training studio

"While there are hundreds of thousands of great SME businesses out there, most will never reach their growth potential or provide the owners and shareholders with the real value of the years of service to their companies. Callum and Jeremy have created an exciting model of agglomeration which provides an SME and its stakeholders with the opportunity to scale, offers shareholder liquidity, and supports founders in reaching their dreams. In this next wave, collaboration models like this will transform the ability of small great companies to reach their true potential and reward their investors. I expect this will encourage and enable much more investment interest in the SME market as its major challenge has been liquidity. The SME panacea?"

Ross Stokes, Vice President Partnerships & Alliances, ETP Group

"Meeting Callum and his team from the Unity Group was an eye opener. Agglomeration seemed to be such a new concept, it couldn't be real. Having worked with them closely, it *is real* and it works! These guys walk the talk."

Gareth G Berlee, Director, Sienna Offshore & Marine Pte Ltd

"Jeremy's book on Agglomeration shows small to medium sized companies how to achieve the value that's sitting in SMEs and how to unlock value that is frozen in the business. Working with family offices and entrepreneurs, they want to be rewarded for their hard work. Without the right formula they may chase the wrong deal, when the right one is under their noses. Jeremy's process for creating a cooperative of entrepreneurs enables entrepreneurs to double or triple their value in one deal and more importantly give them a platform to grow and ultimately exit their business."

Paul Renner, Family Office Advisor, www.paulrenner.com

"I first met Callum many years ago in Bangkok and was intrigued and impressed by what he was doing there. A while later, I found myself attending a micro-workshop on M&A in Bangkok, which was hosted by Callum and conducted by Jeremy Harbour. This was time well spent and opened my mind up to the opportunities and methods that were introduced. Even later, I found out that

Callum had moved on to Singapore and was involved in cutting-edge business there, along with Jeremy, so I was even further impressed with their perseverance, tenacity and creativity. These two gentlemen have written their own books and, coupled with their multitude of experience, have now partnered up to write another excellent book, which should be a must read for any entrepreneur or business-minded person in the 21st Century. Buy a copy of *Agglomerate* and prepare to be blown away."

Mark J. Grygiel, thairestaurantventures.com

"For every entrepreneur who dreamed big but was just not sure how... this is the book. Once closely guarded secrets of the super wealthy, finally there is a book that not only shows you how to do it but also makes it achievable for every entrepreneur and especially the small to medium sized business owners. This book reveals the simple and easy steps to achieve intergenerational wealth and have a business you love. This is a must read for every entrepreneur."

Dr David Dugan

"What goes into this book is innovation at its best! There's so much talk about the sharing economy; Callum and Jeremy show us how even a company structure can be 'shared' for a winning outcome. A must-read for anyone who owns a piece of business."

BoonSeong Low, Founder of Align Group and creator of
the National Workplace Happiness Survey (Singapore)

"This book is a real eye-opener. Jeremy and Callum have laid out concisely why the accepted wisdom of starting a company and growing it organically is *not* the best use of the founder's limited time. That traditional financing options are just not geared towards the interest of SMEs in general. And the exits that founders read about in the news and often dream about, just don't become reality for the vast majority of founders. However, there is hope in an alternative path, one that brings together the best from various funding models and chooses collaboration over competition.

This book is a must-read for *all* SME owners, especially so if you've been in business for a number of years, and feeling disillusioned about the path forward."

Keson Lim

"At last! A common sense book in plain English about how to quickly build a group – and more importantly – equity. It's blunt, to the point and educational. Well done guys."

Denis O'Donnell, XLR Group

"I had no expectations, but this book has blown me away! The best ideas always seem simple and obvious in retrospect and that is how it is with *Agglomerate*.

I am very sure that this concept is here to stay and that we will see agglomeration becoming mainstream. The startups have had their place in the sun and agglomeration is perhaps the next wave. Jeremy and Callum should be proud that they have contributed to that wave."

Anirudh Prabhakaran

RETHINK PRESS

First published in Great Britain 2016 by Rethink Press (www.rethinkpress.com)

*To all of the hard working entrepreneurs
who solve problems, create jobs, and get paid last.*

Contents

Foreword

Entrepreneurship is mostly struggle and pain in pursuit of freedom, lifestyle, self-expression or wealth. I don't say that flippantly; I've interviewed over 5,000 entrepreneurs and asked them deep questions about what they've been through and where they ultimately want to be.

The vast majority of entrepreneurs I meet would be far better off in a job – they would earn more, work less and endure less stress.

I'm not just talking about the lonely startups that never get their whacky business ideas off the ground. I'm also talking about smart people who can sell, people who have 20+ staff and people who have big flagship clients. In reality, many of these people endure insane amounts of stress, experience high-highs and low-lows, don't pay themselves enough and rarely get rewarded in the end.

The media showcases the big success stories and the very quick wealth creators. They love telling the story of the 26-year-old who just sold his app for $40 million, or the young CEO who has a bustling office full of busy bearded professionals working on a 3D printed, AI, SaaS platform.

It creates a narrative that leaves many entrepreneurs feeling depressed and stuck. I've had deep and off-the-record conversations with highly successful entrepreneurs who say that many times on their journey they were weeks away from bankruptcy.

I myself am considered to be an entrepreneurial success story by many and yet I can fully admit to having times where I burned myself out and took my finances to the red line along the way.

When I encounter someone who's very smart, talented and hard-working in business, but they're stressed, financially stretched and disillusioned, I recommend they meet Jeremy Harbour.

I met Jeremy when he was in his mid-thirties. He had just sold another company for a lot of money and had purchased a 60ft luxury powerboat. He invited me to spend time on the boat and at his holiday home. We hit it off immediately as friends but, more than that, he truly opened my eyes to how the game of business is actually won.

Through Jeremy I learned about acquisitions and exits. I learned about distressed acquisitions, deal-making, fund raising and wealth creation. Over the last seven years I've spent a lot of time with Jeremy and seen him win big in the recession, win big when it's booming, win big internationally and more recently win big with an IPO.

The one thing that I also discovered about Jeremy is that he takes people with him. He collects entrepreneurs and he helps them to solve their challenges and play a bigger game. For all of the deals he's done, I have not met anyone who says a bad word about him. He's fair, generous and intelligent in his dealings – although he does swear a lot and people have commented on that!

Jeremy is one of the few entrepreneurs I know who is genuinely successful over and over and over again. He failed very young and he learned quickly. He found a way to play the business game consistently better and more successfully than almost anyone else I know.

In 2014 I was out for drinks with my business partner and good friend Callum Laing and he relayed to me a story about another struggling entrepreneur he had encountered. Once again he had found himself talking to someone who had spent 20 years building a business that looked successful on the surface but wasn't creating a lifestyle, wealth or creative freedom.

Callum is regarded as one of the most connected entrepreneurs in Asia and he knows literally hundreds of people who are considered to be the who's who of business. He's had a similar experience to me in seeing behind the scenes on countless ventures. He wanted more examples of real success in business.

In that conversation he asked me, "Who's the most successful entrepreneur you know – someone who's genuinely making money and living a great life?" I didn't think for long, it was Jeremy Harbour, who at this time had multiple houses and boats and was loving life.

Callum had also known Jeremy for years, but after that conversation they began working together. Immediately there was a chemistry that had all the ingredients for bigger success than either could achieve independently. Callum and Jeremy are both highly intelligent, experienced, sincere and successful, despite tough times along the way. Their skill sets complement each other perfectly and I knew big things would come from their collaboration – I didn't realise just how big.

Most notably they put together the deal that this book is based upon. A deal that would create more than 20 millionaires within two months, be recognised as one of the most successful IPOs in 2016, and redefine what's possible for relatively small privately held companies.

The "Agglomeration" that they created changes the game for anyone who owns a profitable, seven-figure business. Until this deal structure, this type of business was barely saleable because it's too big for a small business buyer and too small for a big business buyer. This middle ground is where I have seen so much pain and frustration. In this space there are countless business owners who are dealing with stress, financial challenges and lack of an end in sight.

Through the Agglomeration model there is a clear pathway to generate wealth from the business, get momentum, do bigger deals, have more fun and make more impact.

This is how the big guys have been winning in business for the last 100 years. Until recently these structures and strategies were only viable for companies with $100 million+ in revenue, but thanks to technology the time has now arrived for entrepreneurs to play and win this way too.

The book you have in your hands is not like other books. This is not a book that elaborates on time-proven ideas. This is the first book to declare that there is a new way to do business that will improve your life and the lives of those you care about. I hope you enjoy the casual, fun writing style and I hope you engage with the stories, but more than that I hope you act upon what you are about to learn.

Daniel Priestley
Founder and CEO of Dent Global
Author of *Key Person of Influence, Entrepreneur Revolution, Oversubscribed.*

Preface

Successful, wealthy entrepreneurs are applying their creative entrepreneurial talent to solve the world's problems.

Malaria is a huge problem in the world and we've seen massive charities and Non Government Organisations (NGOs), with great intentions, trying to fix the problem but never actually making much headway. You've had governments of countries that are devastatingly affected by malaria tinkering around with a solution and it looks like Bill Gates could well, in his lifetime, wipe it out. Bill Gates, a computer nerd from Seattle, an entrepreneur, could cure Malaria. Larry Ellison[1], founder of Oracle and Napster founder, Sean Parker, have both made massive donations to fund the cure for cancer, after being impacted by the disease. This is not simply throwing money at the problem, this is an active involvement in the way the problem should be solved. This is smart money.

Elon Musk has decided to commercialize space travel, electrify cars, get rid of hydrocarbon fuels and put solar panels on roofs. All of these businesses he has created from the wealth he made from his past successes in business. He was an entrepreneur that broke through, exited, got a pile of money and is using that to change the world. Elon's biggest contribution has not been the electric car; it is that he has single handedly forced all the major manufacturers to compete. His actions have transformed an industry.

Gates, Zuckerberg, Brin, Musk *et al*, having made their millions, are now applying them in ways that are solving some of the world's biggest problems with the creativity, resourcefulness and relentless focus on results that we expect from world class entrepreneurs.

---

[1] http://fortune.com/2016/05/12/larry-ellison-cancer-donation/

By following the Agglomeration model we believe we can help give more entrepreneurs the wealth required to start turning their attention to bigger problems. This will enable them to take back power from politicians, big business, banks and financial institutions and be empowered as change agents.

Introduction

If you're the owner of a small or medium business and you're successful, you have probably found yourself with the problem: how do you get to the next rung on the entrepreneurial business ladder – how do you go from being a business runner to a business owner? How do you make more wealth, find more time and grow your business? Should you IPO, the entrepreneur's dream, or should you merge and acquire other businesses? Should you carry on growing organically? Look for funding? How do you take the next step and get yourself that yacht?

There isn't much good advice out there for entrepreneurs like you and us. We're sold the dream of the unicorn technology businesses daily in the press and the myriad business books. We're held back by banks and governments, who want us to keep funding their systems and lining their pockets. We're coming up against the demographic cliff, where succession planning for small business owners is going to be pretty much impossible. Whilst we might be running successful, profitable, award winning businesses, all our cash is tied up in the business; to grow we need liquidity, and who wants to put money into privately owned businesses?

Entrepreneurs are problem solvers. That's our place in the world, to solve problems. So how do we solve the problems of growing a business, get financial and time freedom back, buy a yacht and maybe, solve some of the world's bigger problems?

We can't trust governments to solve these big world issues because, as we've seen from the Panama Papers, many of them lie, cheat and steal. We can't really trust big business to solve the pressing problems of the modern world because they have too many vested interests. Sometimes *not* fixing the problem is their solution; think about the cancer industry, a trillion-dollar global industry – why would they want to cure cancer? On the other hand, a very passionate entrepreneur with a personal experience just might be the person that actually gets the job done.[2]

So if we can't trust governments and we can't trust large businesses to do it, to really fix any of the big problems the world is facing, who can we trust? It's going to be an entrepreneur with money, an idea and passion that's going to make it happen. Throughout history it has often been the case that transportation, medical and even social causes were often spearheaded by entrepreneurs. Of course good people come from everywhere, but even good intentions need a backer and someone who can make stuff happen. Sadly, on their own good intentions can wither and die; add an entrepreneur or some entrepreneurial behaviour and the change happens.

But here's the problem – even though an entrepreneur might have the idea and the passion, they are normally kept poor and don't have the money. Governments, banks, private equity companies, and venture capitalists try to keep them perpetually poor to keep control. The entrepreneurs that break through and make money are the change agents you see around the world.

More entrepreneurs could find solutions to the world's greatest problems if they were financially freed. They can't help the poor by being one of them. If we could liberate entrepreneurs financially we would have massive change in the world – change for the better.

Why is it so difficult for entrepreneurs and owners of small and medium sized businesses to find financial freedom? One of the

---

main problems is the politics of envy. The common thinking is that the people who make money are intrinsically evil and must have taken the money from somebody else. Read any newspaper or watch the news on TV to see the propaganda against those who make money. In reality you only get money if you create value – you have to add something to the world in order to get paid for it. There are of course bad people who make money nefariously, corrupt politicians, greedy bankers and of course even unethical entrepreneurs. Breaking laws, however, is not the preserve of either rich or poor, but of a small subsection of society at all levels, and as we enter an era of ever greater transparency it will get harder and harder for people to hide and move large amounts of money.

Fundamentally, you have to deliver value to the world in order to get wealthy in the first place. The current wealthy entrepreneurs are a lot more philanthropic, there is a much stronger trickledown effect than there has ever been in history. When it comes to making entrepreneurs richer, money is not a dirty word. It has a massively positive effect on society and a massively positive effect on solving some of the world's greatest problems.

Talk to anyone in Investment Banking and Private Equity and they will tell you that you need to keep the entrepreneur hungry if you want them to keep working. We're entrepreneurs and we disagree. Entrepreneurs are problem solvers. They create businesses as a vehicle for solving the problems of their customers. Give them more money, more resources, and they solve more problems for more people. Once they've solved the problems in business then there are many, many examples of entrepreneurs who go on to solve even bigger problems; problems that affect the whole world.

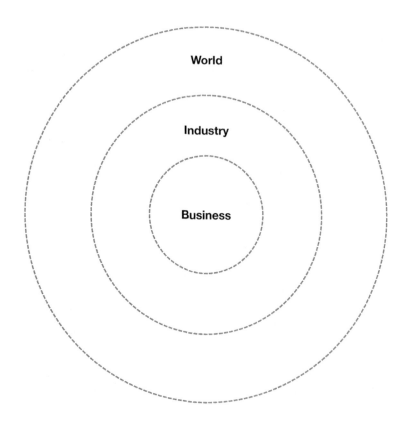

One of the things we want to achieve is to unlock the value that's sitting in these small to medium sized companies – value that is frozen in the business because of all the problems and misconceptions we're going to talk about, like scale and liquidity. If we unlock all of that value, give it to the entrepreneurs who built that value and then let them go out into the world and do great things, we'll be happy.

With the Agglomeration we can help entrepreneurs be rewarded for their hard work, so they can go out into the world as change agents. By virtue of putting small businesses in an Agglomeration we make it much easier, as you're going to find out. This book will give business owners an understanding of the broad picture that is keeping you undervalued and will show you a future where the entrepreneur can scale quickly yet still keep full control of their business.

We'll explain our formula and the process for creating a cooperative of entrepreneurs which will enable you to double or triple your value in one deal and more importantly give you a platform to let you grow and ultimately exit your business.

Who Are We and Why Should You Listen to Us?

With a long career in entrepreneurial mergers and acquisitions, Jeremy Harbour developed a new model: Agglomeration. This book explains the model and how it can be used for business owners around the world. The book is co-authored with his business partner, Callum Laing. These are two entrepreneurs who have focused on helping business owners to be more successful through unlocking the value in their shareholding.

Bucking the trend of the rest of the world, that seems obsessed with start-ups and growing the business through sales and marketing, Jeremy and Callum work backwards from what makes a company valuable to an investor and how the entrepreneur can use that knowledge to double or triple the value of their company.

Contrary to much of the conventional wisdom around starting, growing and exiting businesses, Jeremy and Callum use real examples to show how business owners can unlock millions of dollars from within their enterprises and what the implications of this are for the wider community we live in.

Callum is a New Zealander, based in Singapore, who has started, built, bought and sold half a dozen businesses in a range of industries across two continents. He is a partner in the private equity company Unity Group, director of multiple companies and is co-founder and non-exec director of The Marketing Group PLC, listed in Europe. He is widely published, regularly featured in the media and often invited to speak at conferences.

Jeremy Harbour is originally British, now based in Singapore with a few homes around the world, and is actively involved in buying and selling SME companies and teaching M&A (merger and acquisition) tactics in Europe and Asia. Jeremy founded Unity Group in 1997 and created The Harbour Club to teach entrepreneurs how to buy companies without debt or capital, thereby reducing much of the risk. He has completed over fifty transactions with his own money, and advised on over 200 more in his career. He has bought a bank, has investments in twelve countries and has been featured in the *Financial Times, Sunday Times, Men's Health* and other publications.

With more than forty years' experience between them, the sheer number of deals and more recently their experience of running a successful private equity company, the authors have a unique insight into and now a unique approach to solving the biggest problem faced by most business owners.

If you're a business owner and you have a successful business, or you just want to understand what happens at the 'pointy' end of business when it comes to taking investment to grow or being acquired by another company, then read this book.

Part 1

The End of Business: It's not a unicorn,
it's a donkey with a pointy valuation
stuck to its head

Everything that's wrong with the entrepreneurial 'dream'

To understand what's wrong with the entrepreneurial dream, you first have to understand what dream entrepreneurs have been sold.

When the media is celebrating entrepreneurs it paints them as the modern day rock stars: travelling the world, glamorous lifestyles of private jets and yachts, bending the ear of politicians and ending up on the cover of *Time* magazine. Even if you don't buy that you will one day be on the cover of a magazine, it is quite possible that you have subscribed to the 'passive income' myth. Set up a little business, use other people's money and other people's efforts and you can sit on a beach whilst the money rolls in.

Being an entrepreneur can sound quite seductive.

There are a few types of entrepreneur that we're going to discuss. Have a think about what type of entrepreneur you are.

Hustlers – there are plenty of entrepreneurs like us, hustlers. People like us have always been hustling, starting businesses and trying to find ways to make money. Generally this breed of entrepreneur probably didn't do well at school, always railed against the system, probably broke the rules and felt a little bit on the outside.

Think of people like Sir Richard Branson (Virgin), Michael Dell (Dell computers) and Larry Ellison (Oracle), Bernie Ecclestone of Formula One fame and Sir Alan Sugar, the founder of Amstrad and the star of *The Apprentice*. They all left education early to start their own businesses.

Exclusion can be a great motivator to becoming an entrepreneur. If you're not very good at school, or you feel excluded, it tends to drive you into entrepreneurship because without the grades or networks you don't get the opportunity to climb the corporate ladder.

We never thought of ourselves as being entrepreneurs when we started, we were just using our brains and smarts to hustle and make money from the opportunities we saw.

Jumpers – increasingly, because there is so much glorification of the entrepreneur ideal, a lot of sensible people are jumping out of corporate jobs and starting businesses. There are a couple of reasons, but here are the two main jumper delusions:

The market has convinced them they have to be doing something they're passionate about (see our "dreamers" below), so there's this idea that if you've discovered your passion you need to create a business around it to have the ideal lifestyle. Something the jumpers don't realise is that even people who would define themselves as having the ideal job think that 50% of their ideal job is still rubbish.

A lot of people jump out of "good" jobs because those jobs don't allow them to be "creative". They believe that if they start their own company they'll get creative freedom back. You can be far more creative in a company where you don't have to worry about HR, marketing, operations, making the coffee, managing IT systems and all of the other responsibilities a new business owner has. The minute you throw yourself into a start-up environment, creating your own business, your responsibility goes through the roof, and your creativity leaves the building.

Callum's Boyhood Ambition

Even playing football for England (yup, even at forty years old I still harbour ambitions), you have to deal with media intrusions, abuse from fans and armchair critics, injuries, sponsor obligations etc. Every job has the rubbish bits, but there's a massive delusion around the ideal of "Follow your passion and everything will be great".

Following your passion is probably not the best reason to jump into entrepreneurship. The market doesn't care what you're passionate about, it cares how you can create value.

Dreamers – are the entrepreneurs who want to save the world. Dreamers are "mostly harmless", to quote Douglas Adams. There are many people who have a good ethos and great intentions, and they dream of being an entrepreneur. When their dreams start to take shape they create start-ups.

Callum on Mostly Harmless

There seem to be a lot of dreamer entrepreneurs who have an ambition to save the world or to empower some group through the next app or widget. The challenge with that is they just don't have any credibility. It goes back to my *Progressive Partnerships* book, if you're a struggling entrepreneur railing against the system but you haven't actually figured out a model where you can pay yourself, you don't have any credibility and nobody will invest in you. Nobody will take your ideas seriously until you prove that you can create value for one person, let alone try and solve the world's problems.

A dream will only get you so far, you need money to make a difference in the world. A good dreamer entrepreneur will work out how to make their idea work, and not just wander around talking a good game and achieving very little.

There are good hustlers, jumpers and dreamers. And there are rubbish ones.

Jeremy on Invention

Many people believe they have to invent something to start a business. I speak at plenty of conventions where it's like the National Lottery of Entrepreneurship, because everybody thinks you have to invent something to be an entrepreneur when, inventors nearly always lose and somebody else comes along and takes advantage. If you look at all the great businesses, you'll see I'm right. McDonald's didn't invent the hamburger. EasyJet didn't invent air travel. Virgin didn't invent anything. All they did was take something that somebody else was doing, differentiated it and developed a faster, smarter, cheaper version. Yet on *Dragon's Den* every entrepreneur that comes on has invented something, which perpetuates the myth that entrepreneurs need to be inventors.

To be a good entrepreneur you need to look at where everybody is spending money at the moment and try to channel that existing market, those existing cents, to your bank account instead of another bank account. Much easier to get people to spend a dollar they already spend, than try to get them to spend a new dollar they never thought about spending before.

Why become an entrepreneur – lifestyle/money/passion/save the world?

Plenty of people who become entrepreneurs expect part of the deal to be more money and better lifestyle. However, most entrepreneurs end up paying themselves last[3]. Most people go into business thinking that it'll give them more time and more money, but it takes up all your time and all your money.

There is a ceiling to what you can earn as an employee, so people think they'll become an entrepreneur, break through the ceiling and earn a tonne of money. This situation has changed drastically in the last twenty years. From 1978 to 2013[4], CEO compensation, inflation-adjusted, increased 937%, a rise of more than double stock market growth and substantially greater than the painfully slow 10.2% growth in a typical worker's compensation over the same period.

The CEO-to-worker compensation ratio was 20-to-1 in 1965 and 29.9-to-1 in 1978. It grew to 122.6-to-1 in 1995, peaked at 383.4-to-1 in 2000, and was 295.9-to-1 in 2013, far higher than it was in the 1960s, 1970s, 1980s, or 1990s.

The top employees are making way more money than the majority of entrepreneurs. Thinking of the C-Suite roles (you know, all those clever people whose title starts with C-something, CEO, CIO, CFO, C-3PO) and those people who follow the corporate ladder, not the entrepreneurial ladder, there's plenty of research to show they earn much more.

---

[3] This statistic is mostly guesswork, but we know lots of entrepreneurs and it seems to be about right.

[4] http://www.epi.org/publication/ceo-pay-continues-to-rise/

In his 2013 book, *The Founder's Dilemmas*, Noam Wasserman says:

"... many founders of high-technology start-ups believe they stand a much greater chance of becoming wealthy by launching a start-up than by ordinary employment. If many founders really do believe this, it appears they are largely wrong.

"For the self-employed, initial earnings are lower and earnings growth significantly slower than for those engaged in paid employment.... all told, entrepreneurs earned 35% less over a 10-year period than they could have in a 'paid job.'"

In another study, by The Institute for the Study of Labor (IZA) in Bonn, average incomes for entrepreneurs, controlled for things like education, general ability and demographics, were found to be higher than income for employees.[5]

So, some research says entrepreneurs earn more, other research says they earn less (that's why we don't rely on research, we go out and do it ourselves.) We believe that smart entrepreneurs who are prepared to do things differently, hustlers like ourselves who are really trying to solve a problem, will make good money. But you need to be smart, not just work hard.

In essence, it's not *being* an entrepreneur that makes you the money. It's having a combination of traits and tendencies, as described in the study, *Does Entrepreneurship Pay?*[6] "... as teenagers scored higher on learning aptitude tests, exhibited greater self-esteem, and

---

[5] http://ftp.iza.org/dp4628.pdf - these people have done real research, you can probably rely on their statistics. They also have lots of footnotes, so that's probably good too.

[6] http://faculty.haas.berkeley.edu/ross_levine/papers/2012_7sep_entrepreneurship.pdf - this is a University study, so it must be good.

engaged in more aggressive, illicit, risk-taking activities. The combination of strong labour market skills and 'break-the-rules'
tendencies accounts for both entry into entrepreneurship and the
comparative earnings of entrepreneurs."

This is where the challenge lies. There are plenty of people with
ideas who create businesses. However, someone with a great idea
who relentlessly pursues it until it becomes reality is rare. If you
don't have the appropriate talent, experience, connections or kick-
ass tendencies, you'll stay small, earning less, working more.

So, after deciding you want to follow your dream and become an
entrepreneur, how exactly does the dream turn into a nightmare?
One of the most common expectations in business is that if you
set one up and become your own boss, you will be able to sit back
and relax while others earn your money. But in reality, running a
business and scaling it the traditional way can take years of blood,
sweat and unnecessary tears, with few rewards.

Growing, Grafting and Getting Out

Entrepreneurs don't make money running their business, they make money when they sell.

Tech start-ups and other mass delusions

The entrepreneurial dream often includes growing your own unicorn business. A unicorn refers to any tech start-up company that reaches a $1 billion-dollar market value, a term originally coined by Aileen Lee, founder of Cowboy Ventures. Who wouldn't want a billion-dollar unicorn? Many entrepreneurs are gun shy about going public with their 'unicorn' because as soon as you're a public company, you actually have free trading of the shares to dictate your valuation. If you want to leverage the brand of the unicorn you can't open your kimono when you're not wearing anything underneath.

Jeremy on Naked Unicorns

Effectively, a company is valued at the last price its shares were sold for. What businesses often do, blatantly sometimes, is a capital raise with a big venture capital company, who will put an amount of money in at a sensible valuation, and then six months later put in a small amount of money based on the $1 billion valuation. If you want a $1 billion company, you sell one share for $1 with a billion shares at issue. Then your company is worth $1 billion.

A fictional example: a venture capitalist (VC) puts $60 million in, based on a $200 million valuation, then they'll put in a further $3 million, six months later, based on a $1 billion valuation. They're inflating the value of their previous investment so on their balance sheet the VC firm can make their original investment look like the best thing they ever did. It creates a massive news story around some crappy company that would never get any publicity otherwise, except for the fact it's suddenly worth $1 billion! Everybody goes, "Oh, what the hell's that? I need to see if it works." It creates an artificial, self-fulfilling prophecy – kudos that they wouldn't have otherwise got.

Most of what you see about unicorn businesses is false. In 2016 there were more down rounds (companies that had to raise more money at a lower valuation than last time) than there were new unicorns. Most of them are not unicorns, they're just donkeys with a pointy valuation stuck to their heads. Most of these companies are losing phenomenal amounts of money and are being judged by how much money they've raised. A magazine in our local gym had an article entitled, "Singapore's Top 20 Start-ups"; it listed the start-ups by how much money they'd raised. Not by how many customers they'd got or sales they'd made, but how much money they'd persuaded someone to give them. Using the amount of money you've raised as a metric is utterly vacuous.

There is a disproportionate amount of a media attention on tech start-ups. Obviously, the ones that become unicorns and sell for billions of dollars with just twelve people in an office make great news stories because they are *news*. It is such a rarity. The problem is, you've got a whole generation of people thinking that's how you build a business. We see them on a daily basis, young men and women that come of age and think the way to be an entrepreneur is to design an app, raise funding, get a million downloads, and then they'll be rich beyond their wildest dreams. This is a back to front way of looking at entrepreneurship, which needs to start with the question, what problem are you solving for your market?

Entrepreneurs solve problems. Standing in front of people with cheque books asking for handouts isn't solving problems. If you can take a ten-person company and double it, that's ten new jobs; that solves a problem.

Unfortunately, we've got into this weird situation like a massive echo chamber. You've got all of these tech websites and the whole Silicon Valley ecosystem, which is very sexy and attractive, overrun by people that think what they need to do is to come up with an idea, pitch for investment and then they'll build it from there. Actually, it's jumping over a whole heap of important things, not the least of which is, what's the problem you're solving? Of course there are these *little* exceptions like Snapchat. A favourite quote from the founder of Snapchat, after he had turned down $3 billion from Facebook, "Everyone thinks it's really easy, but people have got no idea how hard I've worked for the last two years." Most entrepreneurs could work for 200 years and not get the opportunity to turn down that amount of money.

Take note though, Instagram was bought by Facebook, Tumblr was bought by Yahoo, YouTube was bought by Google, Oculus Rift was bought by Facebook. None of these unicorns are looking to IPO. They're all exiting to the big incumbent players. This is a really interesting shift in the whole dynamic of entrepreneurship. Instagram could have been the next Facebook and IPO-ed, then they could have bought other companies and been another one of the FANGs (Facebook, Amazon, Netflix, Google) – the fastest-growing tech companies in the world, but maybe FANGI would sound strange.

Now, the unicorns aren't doing that – they're selling to someone else. That's an interesting shift and we have to look at why. A big part of the problem is the complexity and cost of doing an IPO – it's easier to do a trade sale. And from the perspectives of Google, Facebook, Amazon and the other big companies, that's great. Why bother trying to do R&D yourself? They've got all these idiots running around, trying to create the next new multibillion dollar business and burning through their friends' and family's cash in the process. It's much cheaper to watch what's happening and then buy anyone that starts to get traction, than it is to have your own research and development facility.

There's a vested interest for big business to perpetuate this delusion. No wonder they're all starting or funding incubators and start-up pitch competitions.

Entrepreneurs need to solve real customer problems first. If your business starts with pitching to investors then you are inherently trying to solve a problem they've got, which is how do they get a better return on their investment capital. That is fine and it is a worthy goal as we'll explore next, but to start with that is to put the cart before the horse. You need to figure out a real problem that the market will pay you to solve. Then find ways to scale up so you can solve more of those problems for more people.

The most important customer

You need to understand the distinction between customer value and shareholder value. Of course you should be interested in customer value, but the customer that you should be thinking of is the person about to buy your business or invest in your business. The reality is they are two very different customers and they have very different requirements.

Callum on Being an Idiot

One of the things that I discovered the first time I bought a business was that, generally speaking, entrepreneurs are very good at thinking about customer value and not very good at thinking about shareholder value. The reason is that we have to, for obvious reasons. We spend all day every day thinking about how to create more value for our target market, our customers. It was only when I went through the process of buying my first business, not one that I'd created from scratch, but buying somebody else's business, that I truly grasped what it meant to be a shareholder. Up until that point I thought I understood shareholder value (being the only shareholder of my business I was pretty sure I went to work each day to create value for me), but it turns out I really knew nothing.

I was looking at the business I was thinking of buying and I was asking questions like; Why were they continuing to serve a client that they lost money with? Why were they continuing to employ that guy that wasn't doing anything?

The owner, somewhat embarrassed, explained to me that the client was their first ever client and so they felt an obligation to keep serving them even though it made no financial sense. And that guy was his brother-in-law so even though he was useless it would be more pain then it was worth to fire him.

As a first time business buyer I thought they were idiots for doing that. Then I went back and looked at my own company with a fresh perspective and realized that my own company was full of things that made no sense at all from a shareholder perspective.

Part of the problem from an entrepreneur's perspective is that when looking at customer value we typically deal with hundreds or thousands of transactions, so we're constantly tweaking the model. We're constantly refining it. Whereas, when we think about selling our business, it's typically a once or maybe twice in a lifetime sale, so we don't invest nearly as much time or effort as we should in understanding what they're looking for. *Even though it's the biggest, most important deal we're ever likely to do, selling a business is one we are most ill-prepared to make.*

The Entrepreneurial Ladder

Another way to look at it is like rungs on the entrepreneurial ladder. Of course, there's a start-up phase and everybody has to do it. It's a rite of passage, an experience that all entrepreneurs should enjoy. But, once you've done it, maybe you want to move on to something else.

A lot of people think they've been in business for ten years when actually they've been in business for one and they've just replicated that year ten times over like a bad case of groundhog day. The next step on the ladder is to be a business *owner*, not a business runner. Being a business owner is about being strategic.

Jeremy on Being Stupid

Strategic is one of those horrible words that gets thrown around all the time and basically doesn't mean anything. In fact, somebody once told me that you can replace the word strategic with stupid in any sentence and it still works. Try Stupid Rail Authority, Prime Minister's Stupidity Unit or Stupid Planning Department.

Our definition of strategic in business is that your meetings on a daily basis are to do with somebody you are buying a business from; with somebody you're selling your business to; somebody you're doing a joint venture with or somebody investing in the business. Those are strategic conversations. If your conversations are about customers, staff or product then you're still a business runner not a business owner.

We like to explain the concept of making money from selling businesses as:

You don't have to run the marathon, you just have to run the last ten yards and you will still get a medal.

So, when you are thinking about who your most important customer is, it is whoever is going to buy your business. So, of course be customer focused, design your business around what that customer wants, but remember who the customer is. What do they want to buy? They want an efficient profitable cash generating business, which is what you want as well.

Jeremy's Epiphany – Running a Business is for Mugs: Be a Business Owner not a Runner

Building a business from scratch and growing it organically is painful – with the blood, sweat and years involved often far out-weighing the reward. We all start businesses because we want time and money, and then your business takes away all your time and money. But the secret that successful people in business are often reluctant to share is that there is another, much easier way. An entrepreneurial shortcut.

Due to the tedious myth that success only comes from hard graft, people are often surprised to hear that buying businesses, without any cash investment, or risk, can be a much quicker and easier route to world domination. So why would anyone not take the shortcut on the road to glory by buying, owning and selling es-tablished businesses, rather than slogging away in silent, unfulfilling misery?

Most business courses, books and advisors perpetuate the single track concept that business success is derived from hard work, more sales, better marketing, with all the focus on staff and customers. However, to become a truly successful entrepreneur, you need to know when to step out of your business and set your sights on a much bigger game.

I learnt this for myself when I was courted by potential buyers of one of my first businesses; they were pitching themselves to me because there wasn't going to be any cash involved. My telecom company turned over half a million in the first year, a million in the second year and by the third year, it was doing two million. Overall the business was doing very well and resulted in my company popping up on the radar of all the other telecom companies, because as soon as you get over a million pounds worth of revenue you become an interesting acquisition for someone. If you think about it, two telecom businesses have all the same costs duplicated. They each have an office and accounts department, billing department, customer service department etc. But if you put them together, you cut down on costs.

So I had plenty of meetings with companies interested in buying me. When people rang me up I would invite them in to pitch to me on why I should sell my business to them. Fundamentally they weren't going to give me any money upfront, so it was pretty much a pitch of the benefits I would get. When you think about all the things that are causing you grief in your business on a particular day and then someone comes in and gives you the opportunity to take all that away, it's compelling. I admit I was tempted to sell.

If I had met with only two or three potential buyers who were looking to acquire my Telecoms company, I might have found myself in a predicament of choosing the best option for the business going forwards. However, because I met with about twenty, I ended up coming full circle in my decision making process. I realised none of the companies that pitched me were going to give me money up front, which got me thinking about why couldn't I just go out and do the same thing: buy a business without any capital upfront? It was this idea that drove me to buy another telecom business.

This moment was my business epiphany and my mission has since become to humbly evangelise a lucrative truth that is so often safeguarded by those in the know. I went on to buy and sell over fifty businesses, all without any cash investment, borrowing or taking on risks of debt or borrowing.

Fear – Under the bonnet

Believe us when we tell you that every business is a bit rubbish. One of the things that we think holds some companies back is that they believe all other companies have got their stuff together. When you're an entrepreneur, you know that your company is held together with chicken wire and gaffer tape, but you assume that everybody else's company is really well run. One of the fears that you have when it comes to selling a business or joining an Agglomeration model is that you have to open the bonnet, show what's under the hood.

Callum on Buying Businesses

Ever since I bought my first business I have suggested to every entrepreneur I can that they should go through the process of buying a business. Even if they have no money and no ultimate desire to own a new business. The first reason is that it is in doing so that they will likely start to understand the concept of shareholder value much better. The second is that they will discover that everyone else's business is a bit rubbish too.

The problem is that on the outside everyone's business looks great. Ask any entrepreneur how their business is doing and they will tell you that it is fantastic. When you meet an owner that is trying to sell their business and is sharing their due diligence with you, it is only then that you start to see that beneath the shiny veneer their business has all the same problems as yours and maybe a few others that you have already sorted. Don't do this to get sadistic pleasure from torturing the poor business owner, but do use it to realise that all businesses have problems, and that with your new found shareholder glasses on you can begin to make changes that will make it more attractive to a future owner.

It's worth knowing that every business is a bit rubbish. It doesn't matter what particular part of your company is struggling at the time you want to sell; every business owner has something that they're not too proud of, and if they don't the lack of humility makes them unbearable to spend any time with. It is kind of an entrepreneurial maturity, like accepting responsibility, accepting the things you don't know. When you start out in business you think you know everything and any problems are because of some external factor, nothing you could have possibly done about it. After you break through your entrepreneurial adolescence (many never do) you realise the truth in the old Italian expression "The fish stinks from the head down".

The value of time and fun in business

Most people start a business with the ambition of ultimately having more time and money. People are doing a job everyday and they feel that they could probably make a lot more money if they had a business, and it would give them time freedom and financial freedom. Then their business takes away all their money and all their time.

When you've run a business for a number of years, particularly when you get to a certain size, you start to feel jaded. The start-up phase is quite fun because it's rewarding: you can really see a cause and effect from what you're doing. But when you get a bit bigger it becomes harder to keep the momentum going and those game-changing things don't happen anymore. You can win a big contract and that's cool, but you *needed* to win that big contract because otherwise you couldn't pay wages and everything would fall apart.

After some time, and that time is different for different people, you get to the point where it becomes joyless being an en-trepreneur. It takes all your time and all your money.

It's well-documented that it's lonely being an entrepreneur. You often don't have many people you can confide in who understand where you are and what you've been doing. They don't understand the pressures you're under. It's probably not healthy to be on your own with that much pressure for as long as most entrepreneurs. Part of the reason you've got successful organizations like the EO (Entrepreneurs Organization[7]) and numerous mastermind groups that create support groups for entrepreneurs, is because being an entrepreneur is a lonely, and sometimes thankless task.

Everyone has an opinion on your business, everyone's keen to give you advice. Generally, the advice they give is what works for them. It's like saying, "The winning lottery numbers are 3, 6, 15, 12, 37 and 41; you should buy them, because I won with them last week." You'll get a lot of advice which isn't that useful from people who haven't got any skin in your game. It's easy for them to tell you what to do based on their own experiences. Not least, this is because it's hard enough figuring out how you can win at your own business without the introspection required to figure out what could be useful lessons for others.

What you really need is people with a vested interest in your success. People with skin in the game.

Jeremy on Stupid Metrics

All business owners and entrepreneurs are probably measuring stuff. Some metrics are good – apparently what you measure grows. Some metrics are stupid.

One of the popular metrics entrepreneurs are asked about is when they are planning to exit. They'll often say three to five years,

---

which is a stupid metric because it just means they'll be three or five years older. It doesn't actually give them anything. Sometimes people just hold on to their business, hoping it will get bigger. It's just dumb. You're just going to be a bit older. When I've got enough to buy an island or something like that, I can relate to that, but "three to five years" is just a moronic answer.

A great stupid metric is how many staff you've got. Every new employee you hire is another problem. Why on earth would you measure your success by how many problems you've got?

Another stupid metric is how much has been invested in your start-up. Not how many customers you have, nor how much profit you've made, but how much money you've raised.

Which leads us nicely into our next section.

Figures, Finances and Getting Funds

Entrepreneurs make money doing deals...

Fundraising Sucks

You've probably seen all these pitching events where you get 100 start-ups to promise that they're going to change the world and empower an unloved consumer group through the next app they're building, and they get some money from big investors in return. There are incubators to help you grow your idea and accelerator programs to get you there faster. The whole idea is based on getting young hopefuls to come up with the next billion-dollar business idea. It's kind of like foot soldiers – they're the cannon fodder. It's all about getting enough ideas out that, if one gets good enough, you'll acquire them before they get to the head of the game, then you – the financier – are on to a winner.

This perspective is creating a delusional approach to entrepreneurship. For the entrepreneur, unless they get some wins under their belt – and the chances of getting wins under their belt by trying to come up with the next Instagram are insanely small – it's easy to get discouraged by the whole entrepreneurship dream. You end up being poor for way too long, you're not solving any problems and you're not actually creating value for people.

Callum on Start-ups

In my book, *Progressive Partnerships*, I rail against entrepreneurs calling themselves a start-up. What's coming out of this ecosystem, this echo chamber, is how cool it is to be a start-up. Yet, in business credibility is everything. The minute you define yourself as a start-up, you destroy all credibility outside that little pocket of Silicon

Valley-inspired start-up weirdness. Now you know why I don't get invited to talk at start-up conferences anymore.

In addition, most businesses struggle, they reach a point where to grow they need to do something different; they usually need more money. To scale their business, to get bigger, they need to go out and raise money. Raising money really sucks. Generally, you go from being a CEO of a great company and having clients that love you and want to buy your stuff, to suddenly trying to sell something completely different, going out into a world you're not particularly familiar with.

The way the funding ecosystem is set up is really horrible, but the illusion suggests it's a unicorn farting rainbows. If you watch any of the pitching shows on TV or read the tech press, they show that you go and pitch your business idea to a venture capital firm, they make a decision there and then, write you a cheque and you go bouncing off to make your new widget or expand into new territories.

What really happens is that you end up going around cold-calling lots of people and trying to get money through the strength of your pitch. Never in the history of VCs has any business been funded on the basis of a cold call. You only ever fund companies when they've been recommended to you by two or three people you trust. What really happens is that you, the very experienced CEO of a great company, get through the door of the investor and end up having to pitch to some intern that they use to filter out the rubbish. The intern has been taught one phrase, "What's your unique selling point?" The CEO has a company that's older than the intern. It's a really dispiriting process to go through. There are no rainbows.

Even if you get through the horrendous process of pitching to all of these financiers, and you're finally successful, the money comes with such onerous terms that you wish you hadn't bothered. It's a pretty unpleasant process most of the time. In addition, due to the risks associated with a small business, the valuation that they will put on your company is way lower than you would value it at. Then they tie you up in all these knots and tell you your blood, sweat and years are worth nothing.

Why do they put all these strings to the deal? To be fair, they need to protect themselves. Anyone investing in a small business will know the odds of them getting their cash back out are pretty small. Small businesses are very illiquid, and the funds are usually used to invest in new staff, overseas expansion, IT systems etc. All things that can take years to pay back. The investor knows that if they need that money back out any time soon it isn't going to happen, which creates a huge opportunity cost for them. Consequently, the investing companies put so many strings to the deal, otherwise they've got to wait for the entrepreneur to die or sell before they get their money back. Invariably, what that creates is an un-trusting environment. The VC or private equity company doesn't trust the entrepreneur, and the entrepreneur ends up not trusting the VC or the private equity company because of the terms of the agreement that they've made them sign. The whole thing gets off on a footing of a massive lack of mutual trust. It invariably leads to problems.

Jeremy on Trust

Most laws tend to annoy 99% of the population to control the behaviour of 1% of the population. The reason we can't drive more than 50 miles per hour in places is because some idiot parked their car in somebody's living room. The reason that we have all these alcohol restrictions on what time of day you can and can't drink is because there's some idiot sitting under Waterloo Bridge drinking meths.

Legislation affecting the masses for the behaviour of a small percentage basically affects all business deals. Entrepreneurs get tied up in terrible legal agreements, telling them what they can and can't do, to cover for those idiots who don't know how to run a business. We believe entrepreneurs are the best people to make the decisions and run their businesses, and if we just let them get on with that again, the world will be a better place. **You get the best results when you give control, not when you take it**. Bring back trust.

Chasing money, doing deals with people you don't trust and who don't trust you is a fool's game. There's got to be a fairer way.

Depressed yet? You might want to skip the next bit...

You're not going to sell for millions

Most people who go into entrepreneurship have an idea, passion and want to solve a problem. They understand the start-up phase. The problem is, what next? If they have any understanding of the exit at all, it's from what they see in the media with entrepreneurs selling their business for millions. There's an inherent expectation that in a few years' time they'll be able to sell their business for millions and retire. What they don't really understand is why someone would want to spend millions on their business.

Many entrepreneurs, when asked when they are going to exit, throw around the three to five-year timeline. As we've already mentioned this is not a sensible metric. It's just close enough that it's motivating but far enough away you don't have to think about it. When they do get to that point, five years later, they start looking at selling their business and they've got their expectations set. Not necessarily of what it's worth but what they want for it because they've got all the stuff to do that they gave up to get the business where it is today. Not to mention all of the stuff they want to buy, their house, the boat and the cosmetic surgery, lined up in their minds. Then they go out to the market and they discover that lots of other people have businesses for sale, there are fewer buyers than there used to be and it's difficult to unlock the value in a business.

Even if you've got what would be considered a great business – perhaps you're doing ten million in revenue and a million in profit, and you've got twenty staff, which by any standards is a massive achievement and a fantastic business, and you know how hard you've had to work to do that and all the drama you've had to deal with – it's incredibly difficult to unlock that value in a way that the next buyer will see it. So consequently you end up in a situation where the buyer will make you an offer which you know inherently undervalues your business. Or you might get a slightly more attractive earn-out deal but it involves you staying in the company for the next three to five years as an employee of the new owner. Hardly why you got into the game in the first place, is it?

Of course, if you've reached the stage in your life when you are done with the business and you want to sell it, the last thing you want is to end up being an employee for someone else. You won't want to work in the business in order to just get out, so you end up selling it for a lower price and walking away from the business before the earn-out has finished. Data from a company in the US that buys businesses saw 26,000 private business sales in 2015, the average buying price was 2.6 times net profit. That averaged out at about 260 thousand dollars[8], which is a really depressing number.

Callum on Feeling Depressed

The article – "More Small Businesses Are Cashing Out And Getting Record Sales Price, Report Finds" – paints these figures as a good result.[9] I find it really depressing. You've worked for the last ten years building a business and you sell it for just $260,000? Only an impoverished reporter would see that as a fair exchange of value for building a business.

There's so much to think about when you're an entrepreneur hoping to sell your business. Even understanding things like multiples is an important step. Why does any investor invest in anything? Because they are looking for as high a return as possible in as short a time frame as possible with as little risk as possible.

If they value your business at 2.6 times last year's profits, they are making the bet that your business will perform as well as it has last year and that in 2.6 years time they will have their money back through dividends and will still end up owning a cash generating asset. You of course will tell them that next year will be your best year ever, they will assume that it will take longer than that and hopefully you find a happy middle ground.

Once you understand what investors and buyers are looking for, the obvious thing to focus on is to increase profits so that you can get a better price for your business. That might be the obvious thing to focus on, yet surprisingly it is rarely what seasoned

---

[8] http://www.bizbuysell.com/news/media_insight.html

[9] http://smallbiztrends.com/2016/04/bizbuysell-insight-report-2016-first-quarter.html

business owners focus on. Anyone who has been around the block a few times will know just how hard it is to get even a small percentage increase in profits and so is much more likely to focus on trying to change the multiple.

If we use the figures from the article, the average business sold had $100,000 profit and sold for 2.6 times that = $260,000. If they had managed to increase profit by 10% that would have been $110,000 and $286,000. An increase of just $26,000. However, if they kept the profit the same and were able to get the multiple up from 2.6 to 3.6 the final amount would be $360,000. An extra $100k in their pocket. And what about if they were able to change the multiple to 10x? Is that even possible for a normal 'non-tech start-up' company?

Your business is a success and it's still not worth anything

If value is the result of profits x multiple, you can focus on profits or you can focus on the multiple.

Many entrepreneurs find themselves in groundhog day, running the same day over and over, not moving up the entrepreneur ladder. The first rung on the entrepreneur ladder is start-up; the second rung is running the business and then the third rung is thinking like an owner and doing deals and mergers and acquisitions.

So why do entrepreneurs get stuck at that rung? Why are they stuck in the middle of the ladder?

Part of the problem is that there's very little information in the big wide world about what they should actually do next, how they should make that step. All the books are around start-ups and sales and marketing, how to get more customers and how to look after your customers, how to be awesome to your customers and how to get more sales. No one says, "By the way, you won't really make any money running a business. You only make money when you sell it."

The funny thing is that people look at other entrepreneurs and assume that they've made their money running businesses and working really hard. Whereas, in fact, there are almost no examples of that[10]. Most people created a large amount of scale through doing a deal or a large amount of wealth through doing

---

[10] We could do some research and find some numbers for this, but we're too busy going out and doing deals and buying and selling businesses, so just take our word for it.

an exit or a deal. It's easy to keep trying to get better and better and better and better at the things that you're doing without really taking a step back and looking at the bigger picture. Frequently you can't see all the things that are wrong with your own business until you look at somebody else's business.

Jeremy on Being a Broken Record

When I pitch people the Harbour Club it's the first time they've ever thought about buying a competitor. When you suddenly point out that you could grow by a year's worth of sales in an afternoon or you could double the size of your business in an morning they have a, "Shit, really?" moment. Yet to me it's just absolutely logical. I can see because I'm fortunate enough to have been doing it for so long.

I am a broken record. But it's my solution to everything. I always describe ideas as my best current thinking. I don't actually describe it as the wise solution. It's my best thinking because I fully recognize that five years ago it would've been something different and five years before that it would've been something different as well, so everything is in evolution.

(This book is our best thinking in 2016. In 2021 we have a new book coming out. It's a cracker! You can pre-order it now...)

Plenty of entrepreneurs who go into business with the idea that in three years' time they're going to sell the business for millions and retire, get to the end of three years and realize their business is in no position to be sold. Or they go out to the market to sell, but what they get offered, because they're a small business, is so hugely unappealing that they decide to go back, double down, try really hard to grow the business to a point where it becomes much more valuable.

In some cases that happens, they increase the value, but in a lot of cases they've already hit their ceiling of competence.

Jeremy Created No Value in Two Years

In one of my businesses I got a valuation and two years later somebody offered me the same valuation for that business. Basically I'd created absolutely no value in the past two years. That should be a good indication that if I'm not creating value I should have sold.

Many entrepreneurs don't have that kind of awareness. If you're not growing the value of your business, then you should sell or exit. But how?

Callum's Epiphany

One of my more recent epiphanies comes back to the way that you view business. I've already explained how I came to understand the difference between customer and shareholder value as I acquired another business. My more recent epiphany was in understanding the difference between how private and public companies work when it comes to shareholder value.

As an example, if a public company is trading on the stock market for ten times net profit and they use their shares to acquire another company for five times net profit, they then add that company into their balance sheet. The difference between what they paid for the company and the multiple that their own shares are being traded for is all additional value reflected in their own shares. In effect they have just made money by buying another company. The more profit they buy, the more valuable they become.

Of course once you realise this you might ask why public companies don't just go around acquiring everything they can lay their hands on. We will explore that more as we talk about Agglomeration, but in effect if you were to acquire lots of companies through traditional Mergers and Acquisitions (M&A) it would cause huge disruption to your core business and as a company you would find yourself with severe indigestion as you tried to merge cultures, systems, processes etc.

However, when you begin to understand how public market valuations work and you see how much wealth creation goes on at the other end of business, where the investors, banks, VCs and all those guys make their money, and most entrepreneurs know nothing about, it's a real eye opener. When you think about it from a Chief Financial Officer's (CFO's) perspective, creating new stock to acquire added revenue or added profit for your own company makes an awful lot of sense. In effect you create new shares, you acquire a company and as far as the market is concerned your revenues and profits keep growing.

It starts to make a lot more sense why they're doing that, because they have to show an increase in quarterly figures – that their revenue is going up every quarter. One of the easiest ways to do that is not to try and find new customers but go out and acquire companies that have those customers. So that was definitely an epiphany for me, realising how the big boys play the game.

I felt like I had read every business book out there and no one had told me that $1 in sales could actually be worth so much more.

Cajoled, Controlled and Constrained

Your most important customer is the person who buys your business...

So, what are the options a small business owner has for releasing the potential from their hard work and years of labour? We'll look at the traditional methods first, before getting to the juicy Agglomeration model in the second part of the book.

Trade sales, earn-outs and other slow deaths – the traditional exit strategies

Do Nothing / Shut up Shop / Close Down

What happens to some business owners is they get to the point where they want to leave, they put the business on the market for what they think it's worth, the market doesn't think it's worth anything like that, and the business owner has no concept of how to sell the business. They have it on the market for a couple of years, they wrangle to get a buyer and negotiate a sale, and by then they've completely lost interest in the day to day running of the business.

One tactic that buyers often use is to drag out the process so long and tie up the founder's time so much that over time the business gets worth less and so they can renegotiate the price down to next to nothing. By that stage the founder is just done with the process and wants out.

Business owners often end up closing it down and walking away. Any value in the business is destroyed.

Sadly, we'll see a lot more of this because for the first time in history, we've a next generation that's smaller than the generation before them. We've got a contracting bunch of people who would potentially be the natural acquirers for businesses. This is referred to as the demographic cliff.[11] It is particularly noticeable in the developed countries like the US, UK, Europe, Japan, Australia and Singapore, where there aren't enough natural buyers for the

---

[11] http://www.nytimes.com/2012/12/02/opinion/sunday/douthat-the-birthrate-and-americas-future.html?_r=0 - we need to make more babies apparently.

business when the entrepreneur gets old and wants to retire. We believe more and more businesses will be forced to shut down, costing jobs and destroying the value within them. There are plenty of businesses that have been going for twenty years, that are turning over millions of dollars, have great clients, great staff, but if the owner can't sell, they will ultimately fade away.

Sometimes referred to as the whiskey and revolver strategy, drink the whiskey and put the gun to your head.

Pure Trade Sale for cash

Another option is a pure trade sale, where a company or an individual buys you out. This is great if you're looking for an escape, then you might be able to structure the sale of your business in terms of a clean exit, but typically if you're looking for a clean exit, you'll get a lot less value for your company than if you're prepared to do earn-outs.

It's the difference between cashing-out in one go and holding on for a few years. A lot of entrepreneurs who are not familiar with the way exits work have the idea that they decide to sell the business, somebody gives them a suitcase full of cash, and they walk away into the sunset. Unfortunately, that's rarely what happens. If you are able to get into that situation, you'll be getting cash at a very deep discount on what the company is worth.

Despite the problem of the demographic cliff, and there demographically being fewer people, there's also less inclination to acquire companies now because it's so cheap to start your own business. The perception is that it's a less risky option than acquiring something that's established. It's interesting, as you look at the profiles of the high net-worth individuals, a lot of them got their wealth by acquiring companies and growing companies, rather than starting their own companies. When we were growing up everyone on the rich list was from inherited wealth, now there are more first generation wealth creators. Self-made wealth accounted for nearly 70% of billionaire wealth in 2014, up significantly from 45% in 1996.[12] In fact, there's a massive divide between Europe and the United States; the data from 2014 shows that more than half of European billionaires inherited their wealth compared to just a third of billionaires in the US.

Where do Rich People Really Get Their Money?

The French bank, BNP Paribas[13], did an interesting study trying to find out how the 7,000 high net-worth business owners actually got their money. They wanted to understand what the commonality was for the source of the wealth. Did they come from entrepreneurial families, did they come from poor families, did they have entrepreneurial success in the past? The number one factor was they came into money. They got a bonus at work, somebody died in the family, and for whatever reason, they suddenly found themselves with a pile of cash and decided to become entrepreneurial. Generally, the safest way to become entrepreneurial is to buy an established business with customers and cash flow and then grow it into a great business.

Coming into money is the #1 reason that people become entrepreneurs.

---

[12] http://www.citylab.com/work/2016/05/world-billionaire-wealth-global-one-percent/482802/

[13] https://www.google.com/url?q=https://wealthmanagement.bnpparibas/en/news/global-entrepreneuralism-report-2015.html&sa=D&ust=1463728753288000&usg=AFQjCNE7X3buHVHLgzaDwHxRubqs6QpJRg

These days, the perception is that it's so cheap and easy to start a business from scratch, and it's so much cooler to have a virtual website serving everyone around the world and all of that cool stuff, why would you buy a restaurant or an accounting firm or any traditional businesses? So your potential buyers are going. Disappearing.

The upside for a trade sale, if you can find someone to buy your business, is it's a pure exit and you can get rid of the business. The downside is you probably get less value – less money in your pocket.

Earn-out

The challenge is that if you've reached a point in your life where you're sure you want to sell your business, then continuing to work in your business for the next three or five years as an employee of somebody else, is a pretty dispiriting way to exit. What often happens in the earn-out scenario is that they sell their businesses on a trade five-year earn-out, but they rarely last a year because even though they're theoretically still in charge of their business, they no longer have full authority. They have the responsibility to continue to grow their company to hit targets but now they need to go and request budget in order to grow the team to achieve that. All the joy has been sucked away.

An earn-out is the promise of jam tomorrow, that's linked to your future performance. The buyer effectively says, 'Okay, your company is worth $X, but we're not sure it's going to carry on doing what you're telling us it's doing. You need to stick around for the next three to five years, make sure it delivers what you say it does, and then we'll give you the rest of the money later.' As soon as they own you, they tend to change all the rules. For example you have to adopt their reporting standards, they take all the cash out of the bank, and they do all the things to the business that they want because it's theirs. They make it very difficult for you to achieve the results you want to, and entrepreneurs, who are let's face it, not ideal employees, tend to struggle in that environment.

Jeremy on Management

The problem with management is that it doesn't work! In fact most management books I have read in the last fifteen years are all about how the modern hierarchical management structures just don't fit with the current generation of talent. People now want mastery over what they do, empowerment to do it their way and, let's face it, if they have built a successful business why would you want to tell them to do something different? People are too obsessed with control over results. Often results come from giving control not taking it.

So you might get offered, for example, $1 million if you want to walk away today, or $2 million if you're willing to stick around for the next two or three years, with the potential to earn $3 million if the business delivers on the new targets. Then the first time you try and hire someone to actually hit those new sales targets, they say, "Oh no, sorry, there's no budget for that."

Entrepreneurs find that it's quite a bad place to end up. It's like you get golden handcuffs that turn out to be made of brass, and you're stuck in the things for years to come. And don't for a moment think that the buying companies don't know this. Their expectation is that the founder will quit before earning the full amount and thus they will end up with an asset at a discount, and they think through their own brand of entrepreneurial delusion that they can run it better anyway.

Grow by M&A

You could try and raise money, and really build some additional value, because a genuine alternative to exiting is to grow by acquisition. Again, because of the challenges around scale and liquidity, anybody who invests cash into a business is going to want a belt and braces approach to the deal, and then they're going to want to sew their shirts to their trousers to be absolutely sure. They're really going to want to make sure that they can get their money back. Invariably, it looks less like an investment and more like ownership. People get grumpy about the fact that the investor came in and sacked them. The investor doesn't want a ten-year plan, ideally, they want a ten-minute plan, but you can't give them that, so the next best thing is to give them a ten-month plan. Not many of them are willing to be involved for the kind of time it takes to grow a business organically.

Of course by entering different territories and global expansion plans you can grow your business, making it more attractive. Opening up another territory is a great way of driving value and finding new markets, but it's incredibly risky.

When companies sell or merge often the first thing that happens is the key people leave, sometimes with the key customers. In small businesses talent is everything, it is often their only unique selling point. Retaining key talent is a major issue.

Many companies are obsessed with acquiring businesses and changing the name above the door, they want to show off their new acquisition, but with all the years of work and trouble that have been invested, the brand is a valuable asset that should be retained. People hate change, so customers and staff alike can rebel at this point. Retaining a good brand and name is challenging.

There's a bit of an MBA hangover when you do a merger or acquisition, because people think the reason to do it is to get synergies and to centralise, and yes that is one future benefit that may manifest itself, but there are inherent problems and costs too.

Jeremy on Less is More

I have gone full circle on the question of getting synergies when you do an acquisition, born out of my own hard won experience; I now believe, post merger, that less is more. You can spend a fortune and upset everyone, staff and customers included, by trying to rinse every last dollar out in your first 100 days, or whatever plan you are using. Do not forget you create a huge amount of value straight away by creating the scale through acquisition, so be happy with that, and focus on allowing the business to just keep doing what it has always done. Stagnation post merger should be viewed as a raging success! The challenge is how do you motivate synergies later, and the Agglomeration solves that.

Most mergers and acquisitions are either debt funded or investor funded, with either route creating a huge stress on the eventual business, either pushed by investors for results or so laden with debt they fall over (the leveraged buyout, or LBO). You can do a straight equity merger, but you must have a compelling plan. A possible trade sale at some point in the future won't generally cut it.

You could also do a merge and list (IPO), the listing giving you the liquidity in the shares and reason for the mergers. Why would people join a merger unless there was some visible future way out?

Do an IPO

The big one! If a company is growing well themselves, they may choose to do a Market Listing or IPO (Initial Public Offering, when you put your company on the stock market). IPOs have, until recently, been seen as the ultimate end goal for ambitious entrepreneurs. In an IPO you build your company to a point where it is big enough that you can take on public shareholders. This is seen as a validation of the business and allows you to raise money for your business at better valuations. The investors you have picked up along the way now have a public market to trade their shares. With an IPO comes credibility. It should in theory be easier to attract good clients and staff because of the halo effect of being a public company.

The downsides are that the average IPO costs $3.7 million, takes eighteen months and ties up your entire senior staff for the last twelve months of the listing process.[14]

The upside of doing an IPO is that it's still your company. It's the entrepreneurial dream to grow your business to a point that you can IPO yourself. For a lot of people, if they have the ambition to one day end up on the public markets, the conventional wisdom is that you do it yourself. You grow a business that's big enough and ugly enough to survive on the markets on its own. To be honest, this dream is looking less and less attractive. In the US, which has always been pro Wall Street and IPOs, increasingly big companies are choosing to stay private long after they are big enough to make use of the public markets.

---

[14] Best Practices for a Successful IPO - Merrill Corporation - www.merrillcorp.com

Jeremy on One Size Fits All

People who have read any of my previous writing or have been to the Harbour Club will know my one-size-fits-all solution to pretty much any of the world's problems is Mergers & Acquisitions (M&A), and in fact most of the problems faced by small businesses can be fixed by merging companies together and then publicly listing the new group.

However there are a few things to consider when looking at an IPO, not least:

It's very expensive and time consuming, you pretty much need a board to run the business and a board to run the IPO.

You ideally need specialist, non-executives and experienced board members to attract investors. Public company investors are a different breed to business angels, private equity or venture capital guys.

Some IPOs are exits in disguise; all the talent leaves or certainly plans to, so this can give them a bad rap.

Some IPOs are just desperate for cash, and in our experience most businesses raising money are just trying to fill a leaking bucket, so if you want money for a Google Adwords campaign or overseas expansion, it's likely to be a disaster. IPOs are not a good way to raise growth capital.

Most IPOs are pushing hard for the highest valuation because it's either an exit in disguise or they want to raise money (so want to minimise dilution).

Most IPOs forget we are a global economy, and only list in their origin country. Why not take a global view of where best to IPO? I call this the "List where you live" Syndrome.

Summary of the Traditional Routes

	Upside	Downside
Do Nothing / Shut up Shop / Close Down	You can retire...	...with nothing.
Pure Trade Sale	You can sell and escape...	...with a low valuation.
Earn-out	You get an OK valuation, there is light at the end of the tunnel...	...with three to five years of graft, with strings attached and targets to meet.
Grow by Merger or Acquisition	Gives you scale which increases valuation.	Traditional M&A can be distracting, expensive and lead to indigestion.
IPO	The entrepreneurial dream.	Expensive and time consuming.

So what should you do? How do you decide what route to take? What if you make a bad decision?

The Big Problems Facing Small Businesses

Delusional approach to entrepreneurship...

Start-up is exhilarating, fun and exciting, but if the business is not going to die it has to evolve into a more grown up form, and at this point much of the joy gets sucked out for a lot of entrepreneurs. They often fail at this point, move on to the shiny new thing, or get stuck in a desert of mediocrity for years. These business owners are often award-winning, highly talented leaders in their field and yet they still face these challenges. These are the big problems we see facing small businesses and entrepreneurs who want to take that next step on the entrepreneurial ladder.

The Scale Paradox

It is well known to most entrepreneurs that you need to be big to get big. Landing the biggest margin juicy contracts often needs you to be big enough to handle them, so whilst you might have the expertise that no one else does, you often find the dominant market player picks up the contract and subcontracts to the specialist to actually get it done. There was an old adage in the 1990s for IT procurement managers, that, 'no one ever got sacked for choosing IBM'. Stick to the big, safe supplier and even if it goes wrong, at least you can safely point the finger at the supplier and not the procurement decision. It is also generally true in procurement best practice not to issue contracts that represent more than 30% of a company's turnover, this often does not get shared with suppliers they just see their tenders getting knocked back and contracts given to less able, but bigger, competitors.

Scale not only affects growth, but also valuation, big businesses are worth more than small businesses.

Succession

Entrepreneurs are often integral to the business and when it comes to an exit they get tied up in legal knots to be retained, often meaning they can't get their hands on the exit money for years. Or the buyer takes a huge risk by paying them off, then they leave and most of the drive and passion leaves with them; people hate change. So how do you safely transition in future?

Demographics

This is a prevalent problem in the mature economies that have the demographic cliff looming, like the US, Canada, UK/Europe, Japan, Singapore, Australia etc. In these countries the baby boomer generation started businesses, which are often solid, profitable and successful, but whereas in previous generations there was always a wave of new blood to come and acquire or take over the running of these businesses, for the first time in history the next generation is smaller than the last. And what's more, the barriers to starting up a business have dropped to almost nothing.

So, why buy a business if you can start one and compete almost instantly? This means that literally millions of small to medium sized businesses are going to find themselves without succession and without buyers. Too small for the larger players to buy and too good to simply close down.

Liquidity

Although it may seem a little strange at first and is a challenge you had never considered, the ability to buy and sell your shares is a huge driver of shareholder value. Public listed shares often carry a premium for their liquidity, and for most entrepreneurs the exit is a 'binary' choice – they sell or they don't sell. If they take on an investor they have to show a strong business case for the use of the money, they can't just go and buy a Porsche. Liquidity basically means you have a market for your shares which allows you, for example, to sell just 5% of your company and buy a nice house.

Wealth and Value Creation

As a business owner how do you create the best value and wealth from your business? Do you sell, or do you leave it under management? A lot of people had good businesses that were 'keepers' back in 2007/2008 that simply don't exist anymore because of the Global Financial Crisis. But you also don't want to sell too early – what if next year you get all those contracts that you have been saying you will get for the last five years? The biggest issue with wealth creation in business is that only 20% of businesses actually create any wealth for their owners (the rest cease to be) and of those they don't normally achieve much more than a return on capital (sweat equity in most cases). So if you added up the man hours contributed and added a risk adjusted return on capital, that is probably what you have achieved for all the blood sweat and years you just gave up.

It is not just an idea, it is economic fact (ask an economist) that in a free market businesses find an equilibrium where profit basically boils back to a risk weighted return on capital – so the very free market that allows you to start up so easily also makes it very hard to break out from the momentum of mediocrity.

Global Expansion

Having strong international markets and business is a great way to reduce risk and therefore improve valuation, but opening up in a foreign country is a minefield, and can be expensive, time consuming, hugely risky and distracting.

Ambitious entrepreneurs always believe the grass is greener and so tend to go into new markets. The problem is that despite the world shrinking and there being more similarities than differences between nations, there are still huge cultural differences that have to be learnt, normally at great expense, until you understand how to make your product or service work in the new market.

Portfolio Approach

We all know we should not keep all our eggs in one basket, but entrepreneurs feel forced to. They have their shares in their business and that is it, for better or worse, and often this business will be taking the best years of their life. I think we are taught to see that it is all or nothing, that you either 'hit it out of the park' or you fail and there is no happy medium.

Even a "successful" entrepreneur who owns a house and is pulling out healthy dividends from their business each year is often unlikely to have much net worth if you were to take away their business and house. Or worse, they have had their liquidity moment when they cash out from one business and then end up pouring all that money back into their new venture. They are quite literally betting the house. The rags to riches and back to rags again story is a cliché for a reason (and at least one of us might have been guilty of this in the past...).

Access to Capital

Raising money for smaller businesses is really hard, there is a huge sea of capital waiting to be deployed into businesses, but small businesses just are not big enough or de-risked enough to attract it. Of all businesses globally, 90% are small or medium sized businesses, so literally trillions of dollars of investment potential is effectively taken off market due to scale and transaction costs. When you do get investment it is not so much with strings attached, more with ropes and padlocks. You have to sell your soul, your dream and your control to the investor.

Ego / Pride and the Traditional Roll-up

One way that entities have tried to address this in the past is through a 'Roll-up'. The way a traditional roll-up works is by bringing together a bunch of businesses in a similar industry. You then try and rebrand them all to the same name and force through the natural synergies that exist between them.

When you're traditionally doing mergers or when you're putting several companies under one umbrella, ego tends to get in play, because the process tends to be ego driven. Companies are more obsessed with changing the sign above the door, keeping their brand name on the front of the building, than they are about the fundamentals of business which is that you should have more money coming in than going out.

Also the entrepreneurs don't want to feel like they sold out, got bought or gave up, they want to see their efforts rewarded with growth and success in their own name.

One of the reasons why a lot of mergers and acquisitions fall through is that the top level ends up fighting over who's going to be the chairman and who's going to sit on the board. Ivan Fallon, in his book, *Black Horse Ride: The Inside Story of Lloyds and the Banking Crisis*, tells how HBOS was rescued by Lloyds TSB (one of the UK's strongest banks) during 2008-2009. He explains how they were doing multi-billion pound deals that would have created huge shareholder value and they fell apart because they couldn't agree who was going to be chairman and who was going to be on the board.

Talent Retention

On the talent retention side, when you merge companies together and start changing everything you get problems. People don't like change. You usually acquire a business because it's really good at something, and it's really good at something because it has some great people. Then you piss off all the great people and they leave, because it's decided you're going to replace the existing systems and cultures with your own.

Or you try and buy their loyalty, throwing money at key personnel and senior people, overlooking the steady workers who are critical for the success of any merger. Now you've pissed off everyone, missing the point that money alone won't keep your best people. And your competitors realise it's the best chance to lure key workers away, whilst you're busy doing the deal.

Brand Retention

The brand retention problem often boils down to something as simple as changing the name above the door. What tends to happen is that an investor will buy a business that's got a great reputation, great clients, and been doing really well and they'll rebrand it to something completely different, usually their own name; or they'll try and centralize everything so they're managing it from one point, and end up destroying the brand and the relationship that the company has with its clients.

Callum on Killing The Golden Goose

I recently met with an executive of a major business in Singapore. Although they were successful they lacked innovation. They tried to solve that problem by acquiring a couple of young innovative companies. The executive I was talking to had the job of bringing them into the fold – rebranding these innovative companies to the brand of the holding company and teaching them the corporate culture. She was perfectly aware there was no quicker way to kill innovation in those companies but believed that customers would see more value in having their brand on the new companies.

It's no wonder that M&A has a high perceived failure rate.

Management

One of the big problems around management is succession planning. If you own and run a business and you want to sell, you have to sell it to somebody else that's going to run it. Finding that person to run your business can be really tricky. What you tend to find is that people have gone through the journey of growing a business, perhaps from two million to ten million in the past, and will tell you that they want to come and do that again for you. And you want to believe them because they have a proven track record, but really, if they are any good with any ambition, they are not going to want to do the same thing again – they should have bigger dreams.

Hiring someone from the outside invariably leads to cultural clashes and other problems. But hiring someone internally often poses more problems. It is nearly impossible to train an employee to think like a founder.

The other thing about management, is that when you do a traditional roll-up model everyone in management suddenly stops thinking about how they'd grow the business and starts thinking about what their personal role in the new enlarged organization is going to be, so you end up getting a lot of territory fighting and internal politicking.

Synergies and Centralisation

The problem with synergies occurs when people are obsessed with removing the duplications, wanting to strip out all the costs. Again, that turns into change. People are allergic to change.

Most companies merging have a huge problem, they massively overestimate the cost-saving opportunities of the synergies[15]. They spend time, money and energy chasing every synergistically removable dollar and then are disappointed when the cost savings are outweighed by the cost of hiring new staff to replace all the great ones who left due to the turmoil.

Conclusion

So that is quite a raft of challenges an entrepreneur has to work through if they want to grow or exit their business and move up the rungs on the entrepreneurial ladder.

The solution we arrived at is the Agglomeration, which we're going to introduce next. We have done mergers, acquisition and

---

[15] http://www.bain.com/publications/articles/why-some-merging-companies-become-synergy-overachievers.aspx

roll-ups. Agglomeration takes the best from each scenario and makes it work for investors and entrepreneurs alike. The best way to look at it is a sort of collaborative IPO, a group of companies from the same (ideally fragmented) industry join forces, publicly list and then grow further by acquiring more companies in the same space. Read on to find out how.

Part 2

The Age of Agglomeration: Unlock your value and create the ultimate platform for growth and exit

Dignity, Destiny and Getting the Dosh

The juice is worth the squeeze – liquidity for entrepreneurs...

We're living in revolutionary times. More businesses than ever before are being started, technology is becoming a huge enabler for talent, and crowd funding and other innovations are changing the way businesses get started and begin to grow. However, at the "end of business" there has been very little innovation. It is no secret that there are trillions of dollars of value locked up in small businesses. Sadly, the entrepreneurs themselves are focused on growing their own business, whilst the investment banks and others live in a world where risk is the enemy, therefore innovation is hardly a strength.

Jeremy on The Blindingly Obvious

When I straddled two worlds, took my entrepreneurial approach and applied it to the world of M&A, I ended up with a hack of the traditional Roll-up. This, as many good ideas do, appears to be completely obvious once you've heard it, yet probably couldn't have even existed a few years ago.

Callum on Collaboration Not Competition

As I explain in *Progressive Partnerships*, we are moving into an era of collaboration not competition. I am convinced that the single biggest asset you have in a business is your ability to understand and execute successful partnerships. Agglomeration might be the ultimate example of this.

What is an Agglomeration?

To agglomerate is "to form a cluster". The word Agglomeration was first recorded in use in 1774 – so it's been around a bit. Whilst it can seem counter-intuitive that loads of car manufacturers would choose the same city to start their headquarters, Agglomeration is the reason why Detroit became the centre of American auto-manufacturing. Agglomeration is a powerful concept in economics which refers to the phenomenon of firms being located geographically close to one another. These days, with technological advances, geographic Agglomeration make less sense.

But interestingly a geographically diverse Agglomeration of small businesses can make a lot of sense. Our Agglomeration is a methodology or model created to solve a number of problems entrepreneurs face in growing their business and adding value, by which we mean shareholder value, or what the business is worth at the end of the day.

An Agglomeration solves all the issues discussed so far, simply and elegantly.

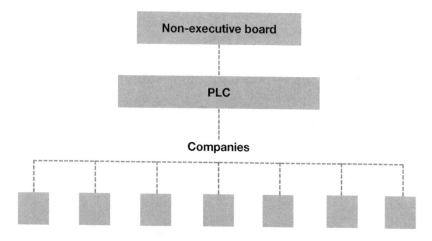

A number of companies come together in a collaborative IPO. The result of doing this is to double or triple the value of each of the businesses in the group, in literally one deal without changing anything in the individual companies.

Fixing the Scale Paradox

All of the member companies share a common holding company – they continue to run their own business in their own way, but with a consolidated Profit & Loss (P&L) and balance sheet in the parent company, giving them the scale to point to when pitching for contracts, as well as the geographical coverage and the product diversification of their fellow companies. They can be big and corporate when they need to be, but since nothing other than the shareholder status has changed they can also be small and boutique when that serves their purposes.

This scale is instant, with The Marketing Group PLC, which we look at fully in the next section. We started with a market cap of 14.4m Euros almost overnight, with more than 100m Euros in additional value slated to join the group during 2016.

Any one of the companies in the group can now point to the group balance sheet when they are pitching for business. Any one of the companies can now point to their sister companies if they need to show they have an international presence, or specific expertise or experience.

Sorting out Succession

Normally succession planning is about recruiting a CEO. This is fraught with problems; employees not vested don't have the same drivers as founders, and you can't solve that easily with share options or equity, as they are salary junkies who just see the shares as an extra that may or may not pay off and it doesn't matter either way. When you review CVs they all look wonderful (I have never read a negative one), in every interview they sparkle, it all looks great until you try them in a live situation and then it is very hit and miss. And a miss is very costly.

The best answer we have found to succession planning is to find an entrepreneur like you, running a business like yours, acquire them and let them and their existing management team manage both companies whilst you sit on your yacht looking at monthly reports and sipping cocktails.

Each business is a silo within the group, so there is limited liability for each business unit, but with publicly listed stock it is easy to go and acquire a similar business to one of the silo businesses and bring in their management team, creating easy natural succession without having to sell out. The company joining gets to merge to make themselves instantly bigger, gets public stock and a better than normal valuation (due to the scale and liquidity advantages). The best way to do succession is through merger, as the best people to run a business like yours are running a business like yours right now! However, the missing piece has always been the bigger picture for both sides and the public company, created by doing an Agglomeration, is that missing piece.

Demolishing the Demographics

For the estimated eight million small businesses expected to hit the market over the next five to ten years as baby boomers retire, there is now a viable exit strategy. Join an Agglomeration and then use the succession planning model to exit out to retirement.

By collecting smaller businesses together, you can create bigger players in each of the markets. Take marketing services for example, there are five or six dominant global players and hundreds of thousands of small talented competitors, by clustering you can create a middle tier and a more stable future-proof business.

Unlocking Liquidity

Having public stock is a game changer for small business owners. As well as being able to actually track their own personal wealth in real time, they now have a viable currency with which to attract senior staff to join them and help them grow.

The public listing, with the Agglomeration model, allows founders to sell when they want or sell a bit and keep a bit. It creates financial freedom for the business founders. The fact that they are all in the same boat creates cooperation on driving share value and the timing of share exits – it is in no one's interest to dump stock, so it happens in a more orderly fashion. Founders have share restrictions for the first year, and also have share bonuses linked to over-performance in subsequent years. To rebalance high performance versus low performance members, this share bonus also has further lock-in periods, which combine to create a stable share price and a natural willingness to cooperate when it comes to exiting blocks of shares.

Wealth and Value Creation – the Holy Grail

In this respect we really believe we have found the holy grail of en-trepreneurship, where you can put your share price on your smartphone screen and literally see your net worth on a daily basis. Your actions have direct correlation – a dollar saved is multiplied in the company's valuation, an extra dollar of profit gets the same multiplication, and every one of the founders around the boardroom table has that same motivation. We take away the binary sale choice, and create smooth and steady exit instead. We also have a dividend policy so all companies in the group issue dividends, which means that the founders get income from their shares so they don't have to sell them to get money. This is also a powerful mechanism for attracting outside investors – profitable, debt free, dividend paying small cap companies are rare beasts indeed!

Another advantage with the Agglomeration is that they get more secure value today and continue to grow that value in a measurable way. They know that the more they work and the more value that they create the more value there is in that stock. They can track their endgame a lot more easily.

Generating Global Expansion

Each of the founders now has a new currency, the PLC stock, which they can use to go out and acquire new businesses to help them grow.

It is simple to add new companies in new territories quickly, giving you a truly global business, and instead of the cost of setup, you now add profit for every new territory. There are huge opportunities for service overlap, tax planning and cost of production reduction when you start to utilise different markets in this way.

The Agglomeration de-risks you first and then you can enter new markets. You can enter new markets while you're sitting around the table with a bunch of people that know those markets and the ups and downs of being involved in them.

Protected Portfolio Approach

Sometimes business owners are fearful about getting into bed with strangers – well, who wouldn't be? We focus on making sure they are not too strange, but we also remind people that instead of having $1m worth of shares in their own business (if they sold it all today), they now have $1.5m of liquid shares (for illustration purposes only) shared across a number of debt free, profitable businesses, so they get a portfolio approach to running their own business. They also get share incentives for over-performance and the share price is a derivative of profit, so they still have real impact over their own wealth improvement, but considerably de-risked.

This is the exact same reason why investors on the public market will value the businesses highly. Small businesses are inherently risky but with this portfolio approach, you will see some businesses thrive, others stay stable and of course some might fail. Overall though, the portfolio approach protects your investment.

Acquire Access to Capital

The Agglomeration is a great way to join the huge amount of capital in the world with the SME sector. We create vehicles big enough and interesting enough to attract the capital and liquid shares so that they can come and go from their investments. The groups also have access to soft loans from the parent that they decide on the distribution of, to assist in working capital and growth projects. Also many businesses would love to buy up their competitors locally or globally, but need the cash to do so – with this model we have our publicly listed stock and The Unity-Group's M&A expertise to help consolidate the members particular niche sectors, or even add products or talent through acquisition. We just have to follow the rules of debt free, profitable acquisitions.

Ego and Pride Recognized

Under an Agglomeration, the business owner remains 100% in charge of their business, the brand stays the same and there is no external interference in what they do. They are publicly listing their business, which is on most entrepreneurs' bucket list of things they want to do in their career, so they are at the centre of a collaboration for a common purpose, and that is a really exciting place to be.

At this point most people in finance freak out and say, "But who is in charge and why don't you push through synergies?"

As entrepreneurs ourselves, we were never particularly good at taking top down direction and we assume the same is true for the entrepreneurs we work with. So we trust them with full control of their business. They have already proved they are capable, they have built a debt free, multi-million dollar profitable business. We are just providing them with a vehicle to allow them to expand that business.

As for synergies, they will come. But not yet, and not driven by us.

Talent Retention and Attraction

As nothing really changes operationally there is no boat rocking to scare off the key people. What's more, the founders are in for the ride to keep working and growing so the most important people are all still around. The ability to reward key people with shares now really means something as they are tradable real shares.

Whilst lots of talented people are attracted to moving from being a cog in a wheel of a big business to being a significant player in a smaller business they are put off by the risk and the lack of remuneration.

With the Agglomeration you can now use the publicly traded stock to attract new hires and give them the freedom to have a significant role in your small company whilst rewarding them with stock in what is effectively a large multinational.

Brand Retention and Amplification

One of our pet hates is the ego-driven roll-up where the investor tries to centralise everything including the brand. It's like filling a bath with a sieve! So much of the value gets lost in the process. Under an Agglomeration all the brands are intact and carry on business as usual, so none of that value is destroyed and you also have a potential portfolio approach to any brand damage issues in future.

In fact, the Agglomeration amplifies your brand and you lose nothing; you are now part of a bigger group.

Management Control

Under this methodology each CEO now sits on a Non-Executive Board of directors, as well as running their own company. They are not directed by anyone, they have statutory duties which are slightly enhanced under the umbrella of a public company but otherwise they have total autonomy and control of their own business. There are basic safeguards, matters that are reserved for group decisions: these are all set out in a founder's charter designed by the founders. The only remit of the Non-Executive Board is to find ways to collaborate to save or make money. So nothing forced, just an open agenda to save a dollar or make a dollar by working together. The majority of the shareholders are represented at these meetings so it is in everyone's mutual interest to make it work.

We also put in place an equity incentivised Executive Board to comply with the markets we are listing on. They are market-facing and include people in compliance, legal, communications and a chairman, plus some industry specific appointments. This board is voted for annually by the Non-Executive Board, so the founders choose this group.

With the Agglomeration model nothing's going to change, carry on, business as usual.

Synergies and Centralization in due course

There is no synergy drive, no urge to centralize. If you come from a finance background this will already be driving you nuts! The businesses are left to nature. The view is, everyone's outcomes are perfectly aligned and that less interference equals more productivity. Most of the value has come from the scale and the liquidity – any synergies are the icing on the cake or pure upside.

Centralization is the most common mistake in roll-ups. There are many examples of centralized sales teams that take years to get up to speed, cost huge amounts to deploy and don't leverage the talent and brands of the group companies. In an Agglomeration the only touch point people have with the holding company is as a public investor on the stock market.

Does that mean we don't wash out synergies eventually? Of course, if you put twenty smart entrepreneurs around a board room table once a quarter they will find ways to work together to save money or make money, but they do it in their own time when their own business is ready for the change and only if they think it will help them.

For example, with twenty companies around the table at some point someone will point out that the group doesn't need twenty CFOs and could probably manage with three. However, whilst every founder might agree in principle, you might have one that points out his CFO is awesome and no boost in the share price is worth having that conversation. That's fine, every founder has full control over their business. Any synergies are nice to have but not the purpose of the Agglomeration.

Comparing an Agglomeration with a Traditional IPO

Let's have a look at the two models side by side.

	IPO	Agglomeration
Cost	Very expensive and time consuming, you pretty much need a board to run the business and a board to run the IPO.	The holding company can be separately capitalised and managed for this process. The Unity Group of Companies provide all of these services in a one stop shop and underwrite all costs so you only start paying a small management fee once you're listed.
Board	You ideally need specialist non-executives and experienced board to attract investors, public company investors are a different breed to business angels and PE/VC guys.	These are appointed in the parent company and incentivised with shares.
Talent	Some IPOs are exits in disguise so all the talent is leaving or certainly plans to, so this can give them a bad rap.	With an Agglomeration there is a clear path for growth through acquisition and a fully vested management team.

	IPO	Agglomeration
Capital	Some IPOs are just desperate for cash, often businesses raising money are just trying to fill a leaking bucket, not a good way to raise growth capital.	An Agglomeration is a group of profitable, debt free companies that basically don't need the money. They are listing for all of the other benefits mentioned not least scale and liquidity. This really puts us in the top 1% of IPOs or probably even more rare in small cap IPOs.
Stability	Most IPOs are pushing hard for the highest valuation because it is either an exit in disguise or they want to raise money and don't want to get too diluted.	As we are not exiting or raising money we can list with a very fair valuation and let the market find the right price, which leads to stable, long-term growth stock, not the roller coaster penny stock.
Country	Most IPOs forget we are a global economy, and just list where they live.	We take a global view of where best to IPO in order to get the best price and liquidity of stock.

So an Agglomeration is not a roll-up, and it is not a traditional IPO, but is it right for your business? Well if you are doing more than US$400k in profit and are debt free, a leader in your field and you operate in an industry where you feel there are lots of similar or synergistic businesses that could benefit from collaboratively coming together to create a major player, then quite possibly yes.

Apart from solving all the issues mentioned above why would a competitor come and join you? Well they are likely to get a much better valuation via this model than a straight sale, and they don't have to sell out, so it really is a have your cake and eat it strategy. It works in any country or jurisdiction (just think of all the public companies you know that have operations pretty much everywhere), nothing fundamentally changes day to day, and it really is business as usual. They get the tools and backing to consolidate their own competitors, if that is something they have ever wanted to do, and besides, business is more fun when you are playing with friends.

Callum on Loving Your Competitors

This is one of the pieces about collaboration that some people get stuck on. If you have traditionally hated a competitor it is only natural that the idea of inviting them to join you in an IPO might seem counter-intuitive, but the reality is that if you are going to lose out a pitch to a competitor, wouldn't you rather that money was still going to drive up your share price? Much better than that the money goes to someone outside of the group.

This model drives the bankers and finance guys crazy because it democratizes the IPO, it dis-intermediates the finance world and gives the power back to the entrepreneurs. When the power is with the founders the advisors are out of jobs. This model was devised by entrepreneurs for entrepreneurs, to fulfil their potential, take back their lives and drive their own destiny. It is much better defined as an entrepreneurial platform for growth than as an acquisition vehicle.

So, let's take a look behind the curtains and see what really happens, with an inside view of The Marketing Group Plc.

Inside View – The Marketing Group Plc

Monopolies are like babies: they're really ugly until you got one of your own...

The Marketing Services Landscape

Companies in the marketing services industry create advertising campaigns, implement public relations campaigns, and engage in media buying, among other advertising services. Major companies include Dentsu, Interpublic, Omnicom, Publicis and WPP. Demand for advertising and marketing services comes largely from businesses that sell consumer products, entertainment, financial services, technology, and telecommunications. The profitability of individual companies depends on creative skills and maintaining client relationships. Large companies benefit from being able to serve the varied needs of major customers. Small companies can compete by focusing on niche markets or by offering lower pricing. The US advertising and marketing services industry includes about 37,000 companies with combined annual revenue of about $111 billion. The industry is fragmented with the top fifty companies generating about one-third of revenue.[16]

We chose marketing services *because* it's very fragmented. What we realized was that a lot of the smaller businesses are all facing the same problems:

- They're doing ok, but not sure what to do next
- They'd like to expand
- They'd like to do more business with bigger companies

---

[16] http://www.hoovers.com/industry-facts.direct-marketing-services.1057.html - this is real research

Most of the companies that we came across were looking to raise money to grow, so they were talking to equity companies, to VCs or private investors. In effect they had all the same problems we have outlined already.

When you drilled down, the reasons they were trying to raise money could all be solved with an Agglomeration. They were trying to raise money to expand into new territories or new markets, they were looking to get key talent on board, or buy out competitors and grow by acquisition. Most of them were looking for capital but were daunted by the terms that came with it. When we presented them with the Agglomeration idea, they realised quickly it presented many more opportunities for them.

The Opportunity

We identified around thirty companies which are all being run by people that were winning awards, were leaders in their fields, were profitable, debt free and doing interesting work. We then picked four of them, based on who got their shit together first ("shit together" being a financial term for getting us their basic due diligence).

The Agglomeration model works best when you have a good spread of companies. Four is not enough, but it is easier to list with four and create the public limited vehicle and then reverse the other businesses into them. Part of the reason for doing this is to keep the market capitalisation of the group low to start with.

First we selected the exchange we wanted to list on, so we identified companies in South East Asia, Australia, Europe, the UK and a few in the US. One of the things that we realized was that we wanted a market that had good liquidity, so that when the shares were listed people would be able to buy them and sell them relatively easily. We also made a conscious decision to choose a currency that was liquid.

What Currency Market?

We'd noticed that there was a dip in emerging market currencies in 2015 which was impacting the liquidity on certain exchanges. The SGX in Singapore and the ASX in Australia were affected. People saw the currencies as being quite a risk and therefore weren't investing in the stocks that were traded on those exchanges because of the additional currency risk associated with it.

We decided it had to be one of the basket of five currencies, as they're known, which are the five biggest currencies in the world.[17] The two biggest currencies traded in the world are the US dollar and the Euro. The challenge with a US dollar denominated listing is that you would end up in the US and, unless you're very big in the US, you end up on a secondary market. The secondary markets are often viewed as a stepping stone to a main market, but more often than not they're a gravestone, not a stepping stone. If you end up there because of the lack of liquidity in a stock, you can't do the acquisitions, can't raise the money, can't do all the things that you expected to be able to do once you were on that market.

Added to the secondary market problem, legal costs and compliance costs in America are just on a different scale. What you can do for five thousand Euros in Europe, costs a hundred thousand Euros in America, even for the same work.

We decided a Euro denominated stock would be good. We looked at a few different Euro markets and again, decided we didn't want to be on a secondary market. There's a nice market called the Euronext in Paris which can suffer from liquidity problems and tends to be for smaller companies. There are a few markets in Germany that are good for tech companies, but they can also suffer with liquidity challenges.

We ended up going for NASDAQ OMX, which is the main Nordic market. It covers Sweden, Norway, Denmark and Finland, and has Euro denominated stocks listed on it. It's a main market so you've got very big companies on there like AstraZeneca, which is a fifty-billion-dollar company, and H&M which is the second largest clothing retailer in the world. Proper grown up companies are listed on NASDAQ OMX (in fact the OMXS30 is the fourth

---

[17] http://www.investopedia.com/terms/c/currencybasket.asp

most traded exchange in Europe), and they have a path that you can take to the main market listing, so you can join on the bottom rung of the ladder and then move up to the main market. Many companies take this route.

The advantage is that unlike going on a secondary market and then dual listing, when you do a secondary market and then list on another one you only do one IPO – one set of costs. Those companies who list on AIM and then go up to the FTSE are doing two listings; so there's two IPOs. When we say it's $3.7m to list, if you have to dual list it won't double the price but it will certainly add to it.

Joining the NASDAQ OMX on the first rung of the ladder, which is called First North and then moving up to their main market is a much quicker, and ultimately cheaper, process. Of course, the markets are always changing and you need to keep up to date, and different sectors may be served better by different markets.

What Country?

The next decision was about where the holding company would be based, which had to be a balance between making it investor friendly and also suiting the businesses.

What we realized was that companies in Europe doing well in Asia are always worth more than companies in Asia doing well in Europe. It's a bit like the equivalent of the rock and roll band cracking America in the 60s and 70s. You really made it big when you cracked America. Same kind of thing now, if you've cracked Asia it is a huge driver of value. We decided that rather than being Asia-focused with European operations, we'd be European-focused with Asia operations, so we established a UK PLC as the holding company.

Now the reason for using a UK PLC is that there are no withholding taxes for our investors, so it means that people from Asia and the US can invest without withholding tax; so we can attract capital from East and West, in a friendly way. Plus the UK is well recognized for having good levels of corporate governance, compliance, transparency, and it's the second largest capital market in the world, so it's pretty well respected.

Who Are The Players?

The UK-based PLC became the holding company for the initial four subsidiaries, which were a UK-based video production company and three Singapore-based companies.

The video production company is called Nice and Polite, which is a great name for a British company.

Nice and Polite – Ross Anderson is CEO. He's the ex-Creative Director of Universal Music, he routinely judges various music and video awards, and he's done Elton John's new video – along with videos for almost every famous pop-star and pop-group you can think of, from Enrique Iglesias to One Direction. The business leverages the music videos to attract commercial work, because all the companies who want to target millennials will go to the guys that are down with the kids.

This creative content agency was founded in 2011. Right from the get go, it has been a well-respected competitor in this particular field, achieving a fair level of success. It provides full in-house service production from anything film- or TV-related all the way to album artworks. More specifically, they work across a wide range of disciplines, creating moving image for promos, commercials and TV and film whilst offering a full-service campaign design team. They pride themselves on being able to deliver a story that cuts to the core of the message.

Nice and Polite has many clients who are key players in their industry.

The Singapore companies are called Creative Insurgence, which is a brand activation business, Black Marketing, which is a LinkedIn marketing business and One9Ninety which is a social media campaign-based business. Those businesses are run by leaders in their field.

One9Nintey – run by an ex-big agency star, Laurent Verrier. A team of more than twenty professionals operate from offices in Singapore and Paris, taking care of social strategy to daily campaign execution, for over fifty of the most reputable brands and customers in Asia and Europe. Founded in 2008 by Laurent Verrier, One9Ninety operates in South East Asia and China through its office in Singapore. The team has an intense focus on business objectives to deliver brand equity, sales and loyalty. They also develop innovative web, Facebook and mobile applications and are experts in social commerce.

The company has worked with many clients who are big industry players.

Black Marketing – run by probably the most connected LinkedIn person in the whole of Asia and the most regular public speaker on the topic of using LinkedIn for marketing. Chris Reed, international best-selling author and the only CEO with a Mohawk, is the founder and Global CEO of Black Marketing. Black Marketing is a premium, personalized, boutique B2B marketing consultancy that was established in 2014.

The company specializes in social media marketing through LinkedIn and creates value to businesses by enhancing personal brands on LinkedIn. More specifically, it creates and manages the

LinkedIn pages of companies. It also does ghost blogging on LinkedIn as one of its services and has proved itself as a key player in B2B content marketing strategies.

Creative Insurgence – is run by one of the top one hundred Indian entrepreneurs in Asia, Aaghir Yadav. The business has won awards from *Marketing Week* for best brand activation campaigns for fashion TV, being experience-makers who bring brands to life. The business creates bespoke integrated campaigns to support B2B and B2C companies at every step from conceptualization to execution.

Bars, clubs, restaurants – Creative Insurgence is a marketing agency specializing in lifestyle marketing with some of the region's biggest brands and groups including Ministry of Sound, the Pangaea Group and the Massive Collective outlets. Creative Insurgence manages many loved brands, including Stella Artois, Jaegermeister and Hoegaarden for the Pacific Beverages group.

With a staff strength of thirty-five in three cities in Asia, they are proud to helm a tightly knit community of 'insurgents' which is an active and evolving database numbering into 100,000, all united by their love for what the brand represents: fun, energy and a good time. In 2015, they expanded into the role of operator. Today the agency is part owner and exclusive operator of the Fashion TV Club Singapore, a 10,000 square feet venue with a capacity of 1,000. Creative Insurgence is currently planning expansion into Thailand.

Then what?

Then there are another thirty companies wanting to join. We'll probably get to a board of directors, *the board you couldn't afford,* of twenty companies by the time we're finished. The twenty companies would have a projected market capitalization of three hundred million euros and we will have produced around thirty millionaires as a result of our activities.

That's thirty of those entrepreneurs that now have the freedom to grow their businesses, solve more problems for more clients, give more talented people great jobs and ultimately who we hope will have the financial freedom to start solving even bigger problems in the world.

The Marketing Group PLC

We called it The Marketing Group PLC: very imaginative. Take a look over here: http://marketinggroupplc.com

The Marketing Group is a true 360 digital agency. Instead of trying to create a business that has only one real specialism, The Marketing Group aims to provide the full spectrum of services to its clients. This is done by utilising revolutionary product silos with market leading talent and services to provide specialism in every aspect of marketing services.

Whether it is a brand activation campaign for FashionTV or Stella Artois, digital e-commerce solutions for Fiat Chrysler, a social media campaign for Adidas or Procter and Gamble, content creation and video production for Universal or Sony – The Marketing Group has the pedigree, the talent and the dedicated resources to deliver industry best of breed services.

The Marketing Group has seven offices serving a global market, with a presence and client portfolio across the US, Europe, Asia and Australia.

Problems Solved

It's evolved a lot along the way. We had to resolve corporate governance, and answer the question of how you control twenty completely independent entrepreneurs. Actually the answer is you don't. What we've found in business over the years, and particularly from trying to do mergers where you stick two companies together, is that *you get the best results when you give control, not when you take it.* When you try and take control of things, you create barriers and entrepreneurs hate barriers so they fight against them. They come up with reasons why it won't work.

When you let them get on with it, they tend to find really great ways of solving all your problems and making everything work. Give them control and everything gets better.

Aaghir Yadav, Creative Insurgence – Being Agile and Dynamic

I was intrigued when Jeremy and Callum approached me with the idea for an Agglomeration, because traditionally my options would have been to sell the company entirely or to sell equity in it, either way losing control of what I had worked hard to build. The Agglomeration model looked like it would provide a completely different solution, with the ability to continue being agile and dynamic and giving us liquidity to grow.

We have a founders' charter that was designed by the heads of the companies. We made them sit around a table and come up with it themselves. It covers how they deal with issues in the business, how they vote for things, etc. They get complete autonomy over their own business. Part of the deal is no one will ever tell them how to run their business. They can continue to run it exactly the way they always have. The constitution is a completely live document that can be voted on and amended by majority vote at any board meeting by the Executive Board.

Chris Reed, The only CEO with a Mohawk, Black Marketing – We Had Options

We looked at various different models to move the business forwards and grow dramatically. The options are quite limited:

Go to a bank for a loan, but they need three years of accounts to help a start-up grow – which is kind of an oxymoron, if you've got three years of accounts you're not really a start-up! It shows just how little the banks really understand the needs of start-ups.

Get bought by a larger company, which has pros and cons; some people have good experiences, others have bad experiences. Plenty of people say they can't stand working there any more when they get bought out, and you can't really expect to be an entrepreneur if you're joining a multi-billion-dollar PLC that has lots of restrictions on what it can do.

Do an IPO ourselves, on the NASDAQ, with the benefit of getting tradable shares, which you don't have in your private company. Then you can raise capital, hopefully increase the share price to raise more capital, then buy other companies to leverage the brand. Which would take lots of our time and resources.

Raise the finance and buy companies yourself, which sounds like harder work than an IPO.

An Agglomeration. We also looked at succession planning because obviously some people want to exit their business, so we help them come up with a path which gets them to the place that they want to get to. What seems to be happening is we get these entrepreneurs that have been running their business for ten years and are really sick of it and want to get out. Then once they join our group, they become reinvigorated because all of a sudden they've now got this big balance sheet to point to, so they can go and pitch Unilever and say, we're a three-hundred-million euro marketing company – and they've actually got a chance of winning the Unilever contract. Whereas before you'd get the scraps from the table from some other agencies.

We created a share bonus scheme that means if companies overperform, they can get additional shares. Effectively it re-balances the books. When you've got twenty companies, with ten of them doing really well and ten of them not doing so well, it re-balances the shares a little bit, so the ones doing really well get more shares. The lower performers aren't penalized apart from the fact that there's a bit of a dilution because there are now more shares in play, so their slice of the cake gets a little bit smaller. Their value doesn't reduce because when people create more profit it obviously drives the fundamental value of the overall company. We put that in place to create some balancing out for the people who really think they can hit it out of the park under this structure.

Laurent Verrier, One9Ninety – Why Agglomeration Was The Answer

I started my working life in the corporate world, for the Havas Media Group, and after almost ten years I decided never again would I work for corporates. I then became founder, partner or consultant to plenty of interesting companies. In 2008 I founded One9ninety and now we're working with Jeremy and Callum on this alternative to a classic acquisition.

We've been approached by large companies who want to buy us and I've done acquisitions myself with these groups so I've been on the other side of the fence. In essence, these deals destroy value more than the create any. Typically, these types of offers ask you to deliver your best year for the next five years in order to make you worth their while. They put hurdles in your way of succeeding, such as forms of heavy management fees, and in most cases you have to move to expensive offices so that, suddenly, your fixed costs have tripled.

Classic acquisitions basically cripple your ability to deliver the profitability that would eventually remunerate you. It might be exciting to work with bigger clients with larger teams and go back to a more global role, but from a valuation of what you've built and the ability to cash out on future growth, I think it's not there. Eight times out of ten, classic acquisitions just don't work.

Jeremy and Callum's approach was an eye-opener in many ways. My other options really were to continue growing organically, which is certainly slower and possibly more painful, or wait until the right offer came in, but the right offer did not come in, even with four opportunities to sell.

Future Plans

This is an evolving model, as all the best models are. We are looking at even more ways to make this Agglomeration model work for ambitious entrepreneurs. We don't think we have everything perfect, yet!

In the future we're thinking about putting in place a poison pill, that allows the companies to unwind if anyone ever takes control of the business and tries to tell them what to do. There's a possibility that a private equity company or VC could come in and keep buying shares from the different business owners, until they have control and then try and put somebody on the board. Under our agreement with the founders, they could have the opportunity to do a management buyout in those circumstances – a poison pill. Effectively, they could unwind so the whole group would just fall away, dissolve. It stops people from ever trying to do it because they'll invest an awful lot of money in something that dissolves

We are thinking of building in this poison pill to protect the business owners, so they can continue enjoying this way of life that we're creating for them, with autonomy over what they do.

Whether this happens or not will be down to the founders to decide, but it shows the level of commitment to keeping the original premise of full autonomy for those joining. We also need to make sure it is safe for retail investors, the purpose of such a clause is so it doesn't happen, but if it does it also needs to be fair to everyone, founder and investor alike, so this is the next problem we are solving.

The IPO

The Marketing Group PLC is an acquisition vehicle with the purpose of gathering successful marketing businesses under one roof. On 8th June 2016 we announced our Initial Public Offering (IPO) on Nada First North Stockholm; the investor memorandum can be found on the website along with regular PR updates. The consolidated group supports the subsidiaries with management and coordinating activities as well as a common operating platform.

The Offering comprised of 1,250,000 ordinary shares sold by Unity Group of Companies Pte Ltd.

The subscription period for the Offering commenced on 19 May 2016 and ended on 1 June 2016.

The subscription price was EUR 1.0 per share, which corresponds to an equity value of the Company of approximately EUR 14.4 million (based on 14,410,000 shares outstanding).

It was 314% oversubscribed.

NASDAQ First North approved The Marketing Group's shares for trading, subject to customary conditions, such as the fulfilment of the distribution requirements in respect of the Company's shares. The first day of trading was 9th June 2016 under the ticker TMG.ST

On day one the shares went up 23%. By the second day they were up 41%, during the volatile first few days while the market decided the fair price it peaked at 2.04 per share and settled in a range of 1.55-1.60, and a market cap around 23m Euros.

Breaking the Bell – TMG.ST

On June 8, our small band of entrepreneurs rang the bell at NASDAQ OMX in Europe so hard that the rope fell off. Nearly a year's worth of anticipation, frustration and excitement was extracted on a hundred-year-old brass bell in Stockholm.

Any entrepreneur with ambition will secretly harbour the desire to ring a market bell on their own IPO. Largely symbolic, it is the moment when your business, your baby, gets to walk on its own two feet in front of the whole world. It is a tacit endorsement that you have evolved your business to a point where complete strangers will choose to own a stake in your future success.

After countless delays and false starts, we flew all four founders and the full board of directors to NASDAQ in Stockholm to ring the bell and announce our listing to the world.

Bell ringing done (and apologies made to NASDAQ for breaking the bell), the champagne was popped and a day of celebrations and constantly hitting refresh on Yahoo Finance began.

We knew our concept was great, and we knew that as we continued to add strong businesses to the group, the share price would naturally climb. But would investors understand that on day one? Had the road-shows, the conference calls, the endless pitching been enough to shift the share price in the right direction?

Glued to our phones and the big screens in the room, we waited until the first price was flashed up. Boom! We were up 16% and trading was strong. More champagne! Over the course of the day, half hearted attempts were made at a Board Meeting and exploring collaborative opportunities amongst the group, but between watching the stock price, sharing the excitement on social media and continuing to quaff Bollinger like it was going out of fashion, this day was one to enjoy the fruits of our labour.

When the bell was finally rung for the end of trading, more than a third of a million shares of The Marketing Group PLC (TMG.ST) had been traded and the price had been forced up 23% higher than it was that morning, giving us a market cap of €17.7m. The four founders were multi-millionaires, and their faith in us had been rewarded.

Idea to IPO in twelve months, but the IPO was just the beginning.

The Timings and Cost

We started it in June 2015 and listed it in June 2016. We think in future it's a five- to six-month process if we really nail it down, but obviously with the first one we've spent a lot more money and time getting the fiddly bits sorted. We needed to make sure that it's compliant with NASDAQ. We've learnt a lot.

The average IPO takes eighteen months and costs $3.7 million and you have that massive distraction of management time. The advantage of an Agglomeration is that we take over the cost and all the management time, and the founders just provide us with the information when we need it. We try and keep that to a minimum. If it's information that we can dig out and put together ourselves, we dig it out and put it together ourselves, rather than constantly badgering them for more stuff. We can do it all for less than half the price of a normal IPO and we underwrite it so the companies don't pay anything until they join the group. Then they just pay a small monthly management fee to cover ongoing costs associated with being on the market.

Are We Joking? It Can't Be That Easy, Can it?

Idea to IPO in twelve months

Why are we giving our secrets away?

We have a pretty aggressive growth plan over the next few years, but at best we can help maybe 1,000 businesses benefit from this model. By sharing the model with others we actively hope other Private Equity firms or Investment Banks will pick up the baton and run with it. There are millions of good small businesses out there that should be afforded the opportunity that Agglomeration provides.

Why finance hates this and investors love it

There's a massive disconnect between available capital and small businesses. Most businesses are small businesses; for example, in Singapore, 99% of people are employed by a small business, if you exclude public sector employees. In fact, if you go to just about any country in the world, small businesses pay for everything. Big businesses don't pay taxes (where they can avoid it) and people who work for the government are just recycling money, they're not actually creating any value for the economy. Everything is paid for by small to medium sized business owners. All the tax burden for the schools, the hospitals, the roads – everything is paid for by these small businesses, ultimately because the people they employ do everything.

Government Hypocrisy on Tax Loopholes

Governments create tax loopholes and attractive tax environments to draw businesses to their countries to do business. They know full well that even if they are not collecting corporate tax they are still collecting tax on the rent that company pays, on all the salaries that company pays, on every supplier invoice, etc.

For politicians to then turn round and rail against corporates for not paying tax is pandering to the masses and unfair to those companies that a few years earlier the governments were desperately attracting with those same terms.

Small businesses are important to the economy. Everybody works for them and everything is paid for by them. Yet it's really hard for them to access capital from traditional sources because of all the reasons mentioned: the risks, scale and liquidity problems. If you look at the overall economy, 99% of businesses can't attract capital, which means the entire capital markets are servicing about 1% of global business.

One of the common complaints of financial companies is that they can't find enough companies with deals big enough to interest them. For example, Berkshire Hathaway (Warren Buffett's investment vehicle) say that their biggest challenge is trying to find enough deals that they can do because the minimum amount they play with is half-a-billion dollars. There's not many companies that tick the box now. They're having to buy into companies like IBM and Coca Cola. They have to buy great big things, because there's this massive disconnect between capital and small businesses. Warren Buffett, in his book *The Snowball* talks about his biggest problem being that he needs to deploy $100 million a week, but not many businesses can cope with that influx of money.

The only way small businesses can get access to capital normally is through debt – they have to put their house and their first born child up as collateral, or something like that. There is more money than there are deals in the world; there's a truck-load of money out there in the big wide world that's looking for a home. There's trillions of dollars sitting in wealth funds, investment funds, sovereign wealth funds and all these kind of places that are just looking for things that they can invest in.

Effectively what we do with an Agglomeration is round up a whole bunch of these small businesses and make them friendly to capital, because now all of a sudden they have the scale, the reduced risks through the portfolio approach and the liquidity of being publicly listed. Suddenly pension funds, mutual funds, family offices, private equity, venture capital, all of those players can dabble in the small business market. An Agglomeration unlocks a completely different sphere of investment.

The Marketing Group Plc is just one example, we want to agglomerate a lot of businesses all around the world, in lots of different sectors. By doing this we will open up trillions of dollars of investment opportunity that just doesn't exist at the moment. Of the 99% of the businesses that are uninvestable under the business-as-normal-model we corral the best of them and put them into investable units. It's incredibly investor friendly – because the companies are profitable and debt free, it means we make the stock high dividend yielding. Plus we price it fairly as we don't need to inflate the evaluation like most IPOs. And of course there is no opportunity risk as they can pull money out anytime.

Agglomerations are a really great opportunity for the retail investor as well. Not only can the staff of the company invest and become wealthy, but retail investors now have some other choices than the typical stock market type investments. Retail investors can invest in entrepreneurial, dynamic businesses that still have the benefits of the larger corporate type entities, are fairly priced and pay regular dividends. So if you want to create income, you can invest in these stocks and they'll make income for you.

Obviously, subject to people's risk capital, blah, blah, blah, blah, blah[18]. They're incredibly investor friendly.

Jeremy on Jetsetting

Investment bankers are dying to get us on a private jet, flying around Europe to meet all these institutional investors so that we can get them to invest in our project and of course we're not. We drive them crazy because it's where most of their money's going to come from.

The flip-side to normal investors is what we, at Unity-Group, do. We're an equity partner with all of these companies, so as an equity partner, we can drive this whole process through. We do the fundraising, the legal due diligence, creating the information memorandum, the meetings with NASDAQ, all the cross-border M&A stuff. All that boring, time intensive stuff, is done by us. This really is the least glamorous stuff associated with being an entrepreneur and it is no wonder many people who start the IPO process give up halfway through – it can be pretty soul destroying if you don't have someone taking over the onerous work for you.

Investors love it because it ticks a whole load of boxes for them but investment bankers, probably not so much.

In effect we are dis-intermediating the investment banks and private equity groups and giving the power back to the entrepreneurs which is of course quite disruptive and therefore threatening.

---

[18] That's the legal bit for you. Remember to always read the small print.

Why entrepreneurs make the best philanthropists

Entrepreneurs are problem solvers, that's what we get paid to do. One of the problems that we're trying to solve for other small businesses is giving them access to their personal wealth. Once an entrepreneur gets the freedom to start thinking in terms of what other problems they can address, which personal wealth gives them, they can go on to solve bigger problems for the world. They can stop obsessing over problems that aren't really that important in the scheme of things and move on to bigger things.

Sergey Brin, the co-founder of Google, has so far donated over $130million in the search for a cure for Parkinson's disease after tests revealed he had the defective gene[19]. He says: "If I felt it was guaranteed to cure Parkinson's disease, a check for a billion dollars would be the easiest one I have written." He has also had his genome sequenced, and has paid for 10,000 sufferers to go into the biggest ever study into the disease, building a big data set that Google will crunch. So even when it comes with selfish motives, entrepreneurial philanthropy can help millions of people.[20]

As an entrepreneur, figuring out how you pay wages or designing that new product takes up all of your thinking cycles. There are a lot of very smart people who could solve some much bigger problems if you freed up more of their brainpower to think about them.

---

[19] http://www.bloomberg.com/news/articles/2012-05-11/google-s-brin-makes-strides-in-hunt-for-parkinson-s-cure-health

[20] http://www.wealthx.com

On a side note, the arts also significantly benefit from en-trepreneurship. As a contemporary example, look at the Saatchi Gallery, which provides a forum for presenting work by largely unseen young artists. Much Renaissance art was funded by the Medici family, the inventors of modern banking.

Expand or Exit?

The primary reason for joining an Agglomeration is for expansion. It gives you the ability to scale, to have partners all around the world. We think it's also a great vehicle for exiting, but that shouldn't be the primary reason for joining an Agglomeration. When it comes to exiting one of the hardest things for the business owner is getting tied into the company. Whoever's behind the company doesn't want the founder to leave straight away. They want them staying around for a couple of years to help with the transition.

Succession planning is really difficult and if you don't do it well you get tied up with earn-out scenarios. For a business owner the worst possible scenario is where you end up running your own company but without being able to make full decisions. You're now an employee, which never goes down very well with entrepreneurs. It's nearly impossible to bring in someone from the outside because you can't train an employee to think like the founder.

The best way to do successions is to find someone like you running a company like yours. You acquire that company and put the new CEO and management team in charge of both companies. Then, the founder can step out into some Chairperson role. That's much easier to do in the Agglomeration model than on your own.

First of all, you might find that within the group there's a good fit with a company that'd be interested in taking over what you're doing. Even if there isn't you've got the public limited stock that you can use. You've got reasons to slowly go out looking for a company like yours to acquire for that exit scenario. You're actually building an opportunity to exit.

Laurent Verrier, One9Ninety – Aspirations

My aspiration is certainly to keep growing the business within TMG; to run more acquisitions. I want to be and I have started to get myself a lot more involved in choosing the next acquisition targets, proposing companies in Japan and China, and bringing solid expertise. That's where I see the company going, not only growing my business.

In this venture One9Ninety is just one of my companies. There is another one that we created, in which The Marketing Group will invest so it funds not only One9Ninety's project but some other projects.

We believe that entrepreneurs should exit eventually, it's a healthy thing to do. We want them to, but we want them to stick around for a few years and grow the business first. One of the nice things about Agglomeration from the stock market perspective, from the investor's standpoint, is that you don't have the succession planning concerns. Often with publicly listed companies, when a CEO leaves the share price dips or it takes a dive. With an Agglomeration that doesn't happen, it's business as usual. If a big name CEO leaves, this in normal circumstances causes stock market concerns. With the Agglomeration model you may have twenty-plus companies in the group, so rotating CEOs out of those companies doesn't have a big impact overall.

The Board You Couldn't Afford

Never underestimate the power of the group of founders, they are *The board you couldn't afford*: there when you need them, but without any control over your business. You have this boardroom of other entrepreneurs whose success is dictated by how successful you are, and the value of their shares rises with your success. It creates a much deeper level of discussion. You suddenly get that community that understands you and wants you to be successful.

Laurent Verrier, One 9 Ninety – The Board We Couldn't Afford

Jeremy and Callum are working mostly on a success fee so they're taking risks. I hope they'll be rewarded as much as I hope that we will be rewarded. So because they work on a success fee, they are a board we could not afford. If I had to pay an investment bank to list my business, it would certainly be at a different price, at least up front. The synergies that The Marketing Group bring us will help us grow in expertise and geographical spread. We've started to work with some of the partners, pitching some very large business. The expertise of this board that we can't afford is opening my eyes on a few things: growth by acquisition, hiring, acquiring, so we suddenly feel stronger. Being a listed company will allow us to attract more talent because we can offer share options.

You get to be part of the board you couldn't afford. You get to sit around the table with twenty other entrepreneurs who have been in a similar situation to you and also have a vested interest in your success.

Chris Reed, The CEO with a Mohawk, Black Marketing – Being Part of TMG

It was a very attractive proposition to work with the three other founders, with Callum and Jeremy the lynchpins, catalysts, of the whole thing. It's great to have like-minded professionals, real entrepreneurs, working with you. The four founding companies are a great team – we're not competing, we're complementary, and going forward every company we buy is going to be approved by the four founders. Callum and Jeremy can recommend somebody but if the founders say no, then they won't get bought. There's a veto, so if we don't think they'll add value to the group we don't have to buy them, and we don't have to add them to the group.

Board Diversity

There is a perception that public companies are full of and run by old, white men. One of the things that we've found out by going through the Agglomeration process is that it is a very closed shop – but the reason that it's a closed shop is that when you list, it's strongly recommended that you have people on your board with publicly listed directorship experience. The stock market and the investors look very favourably if you've got two or three older people with years of experience in a public market. Consequently, there is not necessarily a deliberate attempt to stop boards having a diverse membership, but there is a limited pool of people who are considered to have the necessary experience.

The only way you can break into it is through listing yourself. Once you list, you now have experience as a director of a publicly listed company, which makes you attractive to the next group of companies that wants to come in. One of the advantages that we have, because we're doing a number of listings, is that we can make sure that on every board that we list, we have diverse people who are qualified but may not otherwise get that experience.

We can ensure that we've got some great female board members and their experience with us in a publicly listed board then gives them opportunity to become board members for other companies. We're expanding the pool.

How to price your IPO

The biggest challenge with IPOs is that whilst they're a very useful tool, they're often used in the wrong place. The business press often talks about businesses needing to raise cash turning to an IPO. In our opinion an IPO is a terrible way to raise money. It's really expensive. You go through way more due diligence and regulatory tie-ups to do an IPO than you'd ever have to for other methods of raising capital. Even so, most people do an IPO because they're raising money or they're exiting.

If you're exiting, you want as much money as possible. If you're raising money, you want as big a valuation as possible because then the money that you raise has less of a diluting effect on your equity. You'll really try and inflate the value. Don't use an IPO as an exit or an exit in disguise, or to raise capital. In these scenarios you have to try and get the biggest valuation you possibly can to try and stop the dilution of your own stock-holding when you take on the capital. This can lead to, effectively, an overpriced stock – and an overpriced stock has a tendency to go down without too much reason. A little bit of bad news can destroy the price.

With an Agglomeration, because we don't have to exit and because we don't have to raise funds, we can be super realistic about the price. We're creating buoyancy under the stock price.

Managing the business fundamentals to drive value

As a company, you can control the fundamentals of your stock but what you can't control is how the market then treats those fundamentals. The market dictates the price based on supply and demand. To fundamentally drive value you can do things like reducing costs in the business, which increases profits. If you're valued on a multiple of profit, that has a driver on fundamental value. Margin improvement and sensible supplier agreements that improve sales all increase profit and drive value.

You can do capitalizations, where you take what were previously costs and turn them into assets on the balance sheet. You can do this for research, development and intellectual property. Again, that increases profit, which is a driver for fundamental value. You can also do anything that reduces risk. For example, the Agglomeration model has companies in lots of different silos and that's a risk-reduction method, which is helpful for driving fundamental value.

A negative impact on fundamental value, would be such things as missing your targets, shrinking, or if your revenues or profits go down. Having bad internal controls can lead to bad audits. A bad audit tends to put a downward pressure on your fundamental value. All of those things would drive the fundamental value.

From the market side value is derived from more liquidity. If you have a high volume trading stock, a stock that lots of people buy and sell, it encourages more buyers into the market because they know it's going to be relatively easy for them to sell. That has a market effect on value. Regular communication with shareholders can help influence the market. Most companies list their business but with no plan for future communication – they're so busy running their own business that they forget that they should be talking to their shareholders on a regular basis. Shareholder engagement, having a physical presence in meetings, drives value. This can be particularly tricky when a global business has multiple geographies, but it's really important.

Stocks have analyses done on them, with buy, sell, hold ratings attached. Most people don't realize that unless you're a very big company you have to pay the analysts to analyse your stock. Of course you might not like the answer that they give you but it's important to regularly pay for a stock analysis, particularly with something like the Agglomeration where we're reversing in more companies in the future. It's hard for the market to immediately digest whether or not that's a good or a bad thing. What they will see is a lot more shares being created, but also a lot more profit coming along. If you can pay for an analyst to do a report then that will help, effectively translate that to the wider audience for them to understand what's going on. There are also companies called market-makers, where you pay someone to make sure that there's critical input; they buy and sell your shares. You can do straightforward advertising, advertising the business as an investment and generally promoting it.

Another way to help the market side of valuing your IPO is voting a dividend. There's a point in the lifecycle of a business, where it issues its first dividend, which is normally a watershed moment in terms of its maturity. That attracts a lot of investors.

Then on the negative side of the market are things like missing filing dates or missing key dates where you're supposed to report information. Or ending up on the observation list. NASDAQ has an observation list for companies that are not conforming to all of its rules. You don't want to be on the observation list. Not having enough shares in the open market, not having enough of the company in public hands, can be a negative. NASDAQ has a minimum requirement of 10%. If there's not enough freely tradable stock then you create squeezes in liquidity and when you have the squeeze in liquidity, when no one can buy and sell, it can have a temporary uplift on the share price – but then eventually people lose interest in you because they think if they get in, they can't get out.

What's the formula?

All of these things can have a buoyancy effect on stock price so what's really important when you're pricing your stock is to give it room to grow. We priced The Marketing Group on approximately nine times last year's earnings whereas a lot of our peers are priced on fifteen or sixteen times future earnings – what they might do next year based on forecasts. We really did arrive at the market very fairly priced and that was reflected in our first few days of trading where the market agreed with us. It was a bit of a gamble but we think the real gamble is to try and oversell yourself on your future performance, because then you've actually got to live up to it.

Most people price highly because they only want to give a little bit of stock away. We don't need to do that because we're looking for liquidity, we can start from a much lower base where it's more valuable for us to have an increase and it's very negative to us if we have a drop in stock price. If we did inflate the price and the market turned, for whatever reason, it would make the next set of acquisitions much harder to do.

There are certain "experts" who claim to know everything about listing companies, and talk a lot about "spinning the valuation" so you'd get thirty or fifty times more. They're obsessed with trying to make it worth much more than it is. They're coming from a place of complete inexperience and misunderstanding. Or fraud.

Sadly, many people belive this is how a company is supposed to behave. Of course, we're a small cap stock ('small cap' is generally understood to be public companies with a market capitalisation of less than US$2bn). We start off as a small company, and in the small cap world there are scams and schemes around over-inflating values by either promising some crazy technology; or "pump and dump", where you create so much news around a stock that it goes up considerably in value, and then you exit. These are really temporary strategies. When you meet the people who do this kind of thing they're never wealthy. The difference is long-term versus short-term thinking. If you're looking for a short-term chance to take a million dollars off the table on day one and then run to the hills, that kind of pump-and-dump, inflate and promise the world, makes sense. If you genuinely want to look your share-holders in the eye for the rest of your lives, then actually deliver real value.

In a long-term platform, like an Agglomeration, it's much better to price things fairly and make some real money, not the flash in the pan money.

What could possibly go wrong?

These are the two biggest concerns that companies have when joining an Agglomeration:

- The first is that the stock price is going to tank. They join, they get five million dollars' worth of stock in the holding company, but what happens if there's a stock market crash or the stock drops?
- The second is what might happen if they join the group and one of the companies in the group has a major problem, collapses, falls over, or has a payout disaster (interestingly they always assume it will be someone else's business and not theirs...).

In answer to the first worry, most companies when they go to market the traditional IPO route, are looking to either raise funds or to exit. In order to do so they massively inflate the value of their business. They say next year their company will do amazing things, because they want to do a bigger valuation, that way they have to give away less. They inflate the valuation; tell the market that the next year's going to be the best year ever, then if they fail to live up to that, the market punishes them and the share price tanks.

With an Agglomeration it's completely different. We list for what it's it worth because we don't need to raise money. All the companies we work with are debt-free and profitable. We don't need to raise capital. We're going to market with the lowest possible valuation that we can because we're not looking to raise money. We don't have to inflate the price. We can go in at a very fair price. In fact, we choose to go in lower than market rate valuation because for us the Agglomeration that is listed is now a vehicle to buy other small companies. In order to do that we need a stable or a slowly growing share price – not one that's bouncing up and down all over the place, which makes it tricky to do more business.

Another thing to bear in mind is that the shareholders who join the company become the business owners; the majority of the stakeholders are the shareholders themselves. They have a lock-up period and they're incentivized to keep hold of their stock. The stock is very high dividend yielding, so we'd rather our business owners were taking nice dividends out every year than feeling that they have to sell their own stock in order to pay for new cars or school fees etc.

So you end up with a stock that is as debt-free as possible – the share price should be going up because you're using that in order to acquire new companies. There are not many people selling the stock and there are more people wanting to buy it. That upward pressure should keep the price going up and resist the broader market trends.

Now, there are obviously market crashes and things outside our control. However, the fundamentals of the group – debt-free, profitable and geographically diverse – and the high dividend yield, make it attractive to hold, which should mean that the stock price doesn't have a negative dip. If it does, it becomes attractive to own and therefore value hunters will acquire shares.

If one of the companies in the group fails or falls over there's little impact. Because it's a diversified portfolio of companies it's realistic that one of those companies is going to have a terrible year. We're not worried about companies having bad years. Companies do have bad years, and as long as the entrepreneur is still there they've already proven, by virtue of getting to this point, that they know how to solve problems and hopefully next year will be better.

If a founder is going AWOL, having a bad year, and not helping and/or in the way of progress, the easiest thing to do is to go and acquire another company like them and bring them into the group. That replaces the revenue that's being lost through the failing company and from the shareholders' or market's perspective nothing has changed. You've still got a group of debt-free and profitable companies.

How to do it

We're not bold enough to say it's a piece of cake, but it's certainly not rocket science, and it is definitely a piece of rocket for your business. We have developed a tried and tested blueprint for success. So, here's a quick overview of the steps for a UNITY Agglomeration:

1. Understand the market
2. Numbers analysis
3. Incorporate the holding company
4. Trade shares to founders
5. Yield – ensure that high profits lead to high yielding stock.

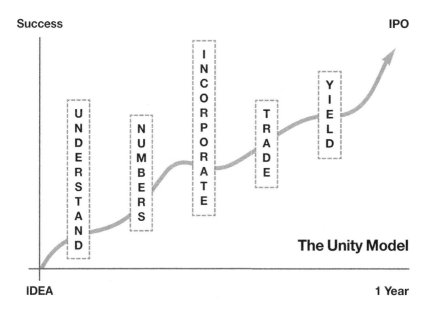

Let's take a look in a bit more detail.

1. Understand the market

The Agglomeration model works where you've got a fragmented market with lots of small businesses that are probably run by talented people, but have reached their current potential. Often times they know that the way to move forward is to use M&A, but they don't know how to do it. We often meet companies that have been talking to other companies for three or four years about merging, but ego often gets in the way.

You need to understand the market. In terms of being able to pitch to other companies to join the group, you have to be able to talk their language and understand their needs. One of the reasons our pitch is so effective is that we understand very well the problems that small businesses face because we've been through them many times.

2. Numbers analysis

Do the numbers. Under our model, companies need to be profitable, debt free and audited. This is a model that's suitable for the top 10% of small to medium sized companies, not necessarily everybody.

Entrepreneurs are great at telling you that next year is going to be the best year ever. We've yet to meet an entrepreneur where last year wasn't that great, but next year's going to be awesome. We're not going to market based on awesome next year. We've got to have some hard and fast numbers. We've got to have audits. It's not the bit that most entrepreneurs like, but you need to get those numbers. Using an auditor gives you professional indemnity insurance that you can lean on in the future. We're either building a massive company, or a massive professional indemnity claim against their accountants. It's due diligence.

3. Incorporate the holding company

Choose a jurisdiction that is transparent, easy to deal in, and is tax efficient to use for the holding company. For The Marketing Group, we chose the UK. At the time of writing this is good for investors, it's an easy and transparent jurisdiction, well-respected in the world so people have a reasonable degree of comfort with being part of a UK company being governed by the UK Companies Act. That choice is a luxury we have by being a global company.

Part of that incorporation process is to put in the required amount of paid share capital, which in the UK is a minimum of 50,000 pounds or 70,000 Euros. Those shares then have to be dematerialized under the UK regulations to an organization called Crest, who hold the share register in electronic form to allow the electronic trading of shares. Because we wanted to list on a European market, not on a UK market, we had to get the Crest shares affiliated with Euroclear, Crest's contemporary organization in Europe. We also needed a trading certificate from Companies House before executing any business within the company. All of those things need to be done before you start agglomerating or speaking to investment banks about listing.

Of course, other countries will have different regulations and rules, but most will be along the same lines.

One of the temptations is to shortcut the process and just join companies into your own company. One of the reasons for having a holding company that sits above all of the companies is there's a neutrality. If you were doing an Agglomeration yourself and you just decided to add companies into your company, you wouldn't feel very neutral and that would trigger all of the ego challenges that come with a normal M&A. There's also risk associated with it, if the holding company gets litigated against for example. It's best to be as fresh and clean as possible so there are no skeletons in the closet.

4. Trade shares to founders

Now you agglomerate all of the businesses in and swap their shares for shares in the holding company. A company has got to give 100%. A lot of companies ask if they can do 20%, sort of dip their toe in the pond, but it doesn't work. The holding company has to have 100% of the subsidiary companies in this model. It puts everybody on the same footing.

There is no greater joy than seeing a founder look at their share price go up on their phone and seeing their smiley, happy faces.

5. Yield (Yacht) – ensure that high profits lead to high yielding stock

Now you're a listed stock, good news updates drive interest in the shares. Issuing your first dividend is a watershed moment in the life of any stock, it will create a shift away from speculators to investors in terms of the profile of your shareholder. The sooner you can issue a dividend, the better. As all the companies in an Agglomeration are profitable and debt-free, you can have a very high dividend plan.

Or of course, you could just go off and buy a yacht! You can now say yes to yachts.

Some pitfalls to avoid:

With every great plan there are plenty of pitfalls to avoid, these are the ones we suggest you look out for:

Don't engage corporate finance and investment banks until you have a ready to list vehicle with all the documentation, all the audits and all the virtual data ready. You don't engage any professionals until you're right at the last yards of the race.

Make sure the founders understand exactly what's going on. Good communication with the founding companies throughout the process is key. Constant reaffirmation of the process. Remember, you're discussing this every day and they're not, so you need to communicate.

Don't run out of money. It's going to cost you more than you think.

Make sure that all the founding companies are going to pass their audits before you involve them in the group, because involving them in the group and then waiting for the audit can be fraught with danger.

Don't be afraid to push back on professionals, as well. This is a new model. We had corporates, lawyers, banks, and all sorts of people at various times try to tell us that things couldn't be done this particular way.

Strategic (stupid) advice costs millions

One lawyer told their client, "Absolutely don't do it." That cost their client three and a half million euros. This was not a securities lawyer, so the advice to that company was unqualified. Another lawyer asked, "Are you going to do a group of lawyers? I want to join one." The difference between professionals getting this and not getting this is really quite dramatic.

This whole Agglomeration process can function without lawyers and accountants. Yes, you need audited accounts and legal sign off on the stuff to do with the IPO, but you don't need it for the sale and purchase agreements. You don't need lawyers for a lot of the stuff. You can get rid of the traditional advisors who don't really add any value to the process.

Are you ready for an Agglomeration?

An Agglomeration isn't for every business. You might be better off with a traditional M&A or IPO. Find out if an Agglomeration is right for you by answering the following questions:

- Do you have at least $400k in profit?
- Are you debt free?
- Are you a leader in your field, and have won awards and plaudits?
- Do you operate in an industry where you feel there are lots of similar or synergistic businesses that could benefit from collaboratively coming together to create a major player?
- Are you willing to work collaboratively with other people?

If you answered yes to all of these questions an Agglomeration could be for you. However, it really depends on your plans and desires for the future, and what type of person you are:

- Are you looking for an exit?
- Do you want to retire within the next twelve months?
- Are you a bit of an asshole?

If you answered yes to these questions then maybe an Agglomeration isn't the right vehicle for you. An Agglomeration is more of an incubation for smart entrepreneurs than an exit.

Conclusion

Many good things in the world come from an entrepreneur's innovation and ability to make stuff happen: diseases have been cured, solutions to the world's transport and ecological problems have been discovered, Facebook was launched(!) – all these solutions have been and are being driven by entrepreneurs. Entrepreneurs have their special projects, the problems they want to fix, whether it's making sure that nobody starves to death, ensuring that everybody has clean drinking water or searching for world peace. That's the life of an entrepreneur – to solve problems.

Entrepreneurs are the people in this world who make things happen, but traditionally it is only a tiny few that manage to crack through to see huge success and huge impact.

An Agglomeration is a unique approach that is dis-intermediating the banks and financial institutions and giving the power back to entrepreneurs.

Whilst many aspects of the model are being used by others, Unity-Group is the first to put all the elements together in a way that serves the business owner rather than the financial institutions.

Agglomeration shows how normal business owners, across all business sectors, can come together to use the capital markets for what they were originally intended: funding the growth of great businesses that are creating real value in the world for their clients and the wider community.

To be a wealthy, successful entrepreneur you don't need to invent the next unicorn business; leave that to the kids. We believe that if you can help good, debt-free, profitable businesses grow from one million to ten million, or ten million to a hundred million, you'd make a far bigger contribution to the world.

Every time we do an Agglomeration, 1% of the shares gets put into a charitable trust in the name of the company, to be overseen and managed by somebody worthy. We work with the Buy1Give1 organization – www.b1g1.com – that helps small and medium sized businesses achieve more social impact by embedding giving activities in their everyday business operations.

Our reason for sharing this strategy in this book is that we would love to see more businesses have the chance to scale faster, hire more people, serve more clients, and ultimately leave the founders with a wealth that can have an even more positive impact on the World.

We hope it has shown you a new path and one that will afford you much success. Go #agglomerate!

Acknowledgements

Thanks to:

The team at Unity Group in Singapore who work so hard to let us do what we do best.

Our partners and collaborators around the world.

Debs and the team at Rethink Press.

From Jeremy to Simona, Ariella J Harbour, and the one in the oven.

From Callum to Zo, Mia and Ella.

The Authors

Callum Laing (left) and Jeremy Harbour (right)

Jeremy Harbour

Jeremy is a leading expert in the field of Mergers & Acquisitions in Europe, the USA and in Asia. Based out of Singapore but with a global focus, he owns investments in twelve countries, has bought and sold over fifty companies, and advised on around 200 more. He is also the Advisory Director of The Mint National Bank.

Lecturing all over the world on the subject of SME M&A with a focus on distressed and motivated acquisitions, Jeremy has coached people from numerous larger organisations, including Moore Stevens, KPMG, Tesco and Microsoft, on how to buy small to medium sized companies. He is an avid keynote speaker and has spoken at numerous events with audience sizes of up to 700.

He is three-times runner up Coutts Entrepreneur of the Year in the UK, has provided mentoring to The Prince's Trust, and has been invited to Buckingham Palace and The British Houses of Parliament to advise on matters of business and enterprise. He has been featured in *The Sunday Times, Financial Times*, and numerous other publications; he has also appeared on The Money Channel. Jeremy is the founder of Unity-Group and the mind behind the Agglomeration Model.

Callum Laing

Callum has started, built, bought and sold half a dozen businesses in a range of industries across two continents. He is a partner in the Unity-Group, co-founder and non-exec director of The Marketing Group and is also a Director of Dent Asia.

Callum is the author of *Progressive Partnerships – The Future of Business* and publishes a daily interview with business leaders and entrepreneurs in Asia on Asianentrepreneur.org

A regular speaker at conferences on entrepreneurship and other business topics, Callum is regularly featured on TV and in the press.

His enterprise experiences range from Recruitment to Sailing Regattas and from Employee Engagement to Nightclubs.

How The Unity Group Can Help

Website www.Unity-Group.com / http://marketinggroupplc.com/

Get in touch
https://www.linkedin.com/in/callumlaing
https://www.linkedin.com/in/jeremyharbour
@laingcallum
@unitygroup